THE APOSTOLIC IMPERATIVE

Nature and Aim of the Church's Mission and Ministry

CARL E. BRAATEN

AUGSBURG Publishing House • Minneapolis

To my wife
LaVonne

THE APOSTOLIC IMPERATIVE
Nature and Aim of the Church's Mission and Ministry

Copyright © 1985 Augsburg Publishing House

Scripture quotations unless otherwise noted are from the Revised Standard Version of the Bible, copyright 1946, 1952, and 1971 by the Division of Christian Education of the National Council of Churches.

Library of Congress Cataloging in Publication Data

Braaten, Carl E., 1929-
  THE APOSTOLIC IMPERATIVE.

  Bibliography: p.
  1. Mission of the church.   2. Clergy—Office.
3. Lutheran Church—Doctrines.   I. Title.
BV601.8.B675   1985   260   85-7526
ISBN 0-8066-2168-0

Manufactured in the U.S.A.   APH 10-0410

1   2   3   4   5   6   7   8   9   0   1   2   3   4   5   6   7   8   9

CONTENTS

ACKNOWLEDGMENTS

Chapter 1 was delivered at Regis College, Toronto, as the Chancellor's Address, November 21, 1983; Chapter 3 appeared in *Currents in Theology and Mission* 10:4 (August 1983); Chapter 6 was published in *dialog* 24 (Fall 1984).

INTRODUCTION:

The Church's Mission and the Crises of Our Time

The church in mission confronts two major crises that threaten the life and well-being of millions, even billions, of people today. The first is the existential crisis of meaning, and the second is the global crisis of misery. The existential crisis of meaning has become epidemic in the midst of Western affluence. It is related to drugs and alcohol, the punkers' protest and the increasing rate of suicide. We live within a culture suffering from neurotic self-disintegration in the wake of a collapsed Christian Weltanschauung. We search for meaning, even the meaning of meaning. We experience life in broken bits and pieces, without relation to a larger whole that establishes the condition of their meaning. One experience or one moment is episodic, and does not release its own meaning. The crisis of meaning arises because people experience their lives in fragments without being related to a goal with finality of meaning. The collapsed sense of the whole robs the events of experience of the necessary condition of their meaning. The myths that used to envelop life and enshrine meaning have been eroded.

People who suffer the crisis of misery are often too poor to experience the existential crisis of meaning. The pain in the gut is so great that the nervous system does not function well enough to register the more sophisticated human "sickness unto death," things like angst and ennui. The numbers of miserably wretched people on earth are growing. Wars are being fought by nations to secure their hand on the bread knife. Millions will die of starvation and war. There is a crisis in the modern experience of objective reality that seems far beyond our control. We see it happening in terms of class conflicts in society and the many situations of injustice, poverty, and oppression, through which masses of people are dehumanized by demonic systems. On top of all this misery hangs the fear of the mushroom cloud that might punctuate every kind of misery with an apocalyptic bang.

If Christians act on their own faith-assumptions, they will not respond to the crises of our time with feelings of paralysis, indifference, panic, or hysteria. "Now when these things begin to take place, look up and raise your heads, because your redemption is drawing near" (Luke 21:28). When Luther was supposedly asked what he would do if he knew the world were to end tomorrow, he answered, "I would go out and plant a tree." This does not mean that we should carry on like an ostrich, as though nothing is happening in the world to which we must respond.

The challenge that faces a hermeneutic of mission is to show that the God of the Bible, the Father of Jesus the Messiah, discloses the totality of meaning in God's self-revelation adequate to each individual's quest for the meaning of life. This God is revealing the eschatological future of all reality, and therewith the final meaning of the events of our personal experience and of the world in general. This idea that the meaning of life in history depends on a total framework of meaning is based on the chief religious symbol of the biblical-Christian faith—the kingdom of God. The kingdom of God was the central motif of Jesus' ministry and proclamation, and he alone provides the hinge on which both Testaments swing.

The church's response to the crisis of meaning must meet the challenge at several levels—intellectual, moral, and religious. The breakdown of the structures of meaning is pervasive. Intellectually, we must be about restoring in an authentic way the basic vision of God and the world mediated by the central symbols of the Christian faith under the conditions of modern ways of thinking, which include but are not exclusively reducible to scientific hypotheses about the nature of the world and humanity. Christianity does make cognitive claims, and where these are not attended to, a crisis of belief can become the occasion for the deeper crisis of meaning. Some people can endure the crisis of belief and appear to function as healthy secular-minded people. This appearance nourished Bonhoeffer's myth about the "world come of age" in which healthy secularists seem to live with no religious sense of existential lack or need of dependence on God.

In addition to the intellectual dimension of the modern crisis of meaning, there is the crisis of morality. Almost every major Christian ethical norm, ideal, value, or virtue has been called into question, not only by people outside the Christian community but also by some within it. Ethical models and ethical commitments are being dictated by a culture which has now reached an advanced stage of neopaganism, although the outer shell of civilized society seems relatively intact. There are new gods, or perhaps only new masks of the old demons. The moral content of the sacred texts and classic traditions no longer possesses any substantial authority. The chaos in Christian ethics has reached crisis proportions, and we are doing very little about it. Our basic posture is culture-conforming. Eventually, this will bring about a swing of the pendulum back to the past and generate a return to a repristinating legalism in ethics as it does to a repristinating fundamentalism in doctrine. Neither stance is acceptable to Lutherans who have been liberated by the gospel, but not so as to continue in sin that grace may abound. Confusion abounds on the issues of law and gospel, sin and grace, justification and sanctification, faith and works.

The cognitive crisis of belief and the moral dilemmas feed the religious dimension of the crisis of meaning. People are not merely troubled by the cognitive claims to theological truth, nor are they merely facing moral uncertainty in face of ethical relativism. They are also experiencing the erosion of religious substance mediated through the rites and symbols of the faith, in family life and public worship. We should give our theology a hermeneutical checkup to determine whether we are adequately meeting these three dimensions of the crisis of meaning—intellectual, moral, and religious. A failure to mediate the core and content of the Christian faith in lively forms of interpretation today at any one of the three levels of crisis will mean that we are dealing with something less than the whole person.

When we turn to the social dimension of crisis which bears on objective reality in political and economic terms, the church in mission appears relatively helpless, but not at all unwilling to participate in the challenges of our time. If one would examine various parts of the church today—its institutions, congregations, synodical statements, and theological formulations—and compare them to where the church was 20 years ago, one would find a shift of emphasis from chiefly intraecclesial concerns to new frontiers beyond the walls of the church. The concept of practical theology today has been vastly broadened to include the practical-critical activity of the church in the world. The entire mission program of the church incorporates solidarity with victims, strategies to deal with issues causing poverty and oppression, and concerns for peace and justice of international scope. All of these trends reflect a new awareness within the church that the modern crisis is not only soteriological (Luther's question) but also sociological (Marx's question).

The church in mission seems inadequately equipped to function on the basis of a political hermeneutics of the gospel. Various forms of liberation theology are calling our attention to the truth that ''pure doctrine'' is not meant to be an end in itself, but must relate critically to the practice of faith. This notion that theology and practice must go together for either to be credible need not be bound to the Marxist concept of *praxis*. We should be challenged by Marxism to go more deeply into a Christian understanding of practice—''doing the truth in love''! In the best tradition, theology was a ''*habitus practicus.*'' This means that to be true to its very nature theology must be operationally effective and productive of concrete acts. The result of our theological work is not holding a new set of abstract ideas in our heads but a commitment to participate in God's call and mission to change the world in concrete ways. Theology should be a tool of freedom—personal, communal, cultural, and political; it should be a means to the end of the sort of ecclesial praxis that will deal with hunger, poverty, and material misery of every kind.

Theology has developed the concept of holistic mission to meet the challenges of our time. It overcomes a certain onesidedness that placed all the emphasis on personal evangelism and planting churches. On the other hand, the idea of holistic mission has contributed to such a great inflation in the meaning of mission, including virtually everything the church is doing, that there is the danger that evangelism, which is the heart of mission, will become buried in an avalanche of church activism, under the controls of a burgeoning bureaucracy. The occupational hazard of *talking* about rather than *being* about the evangelistic task strikes the church in its most vulnerable spot.

"Mission" rightly understood has a broader meaning than "evangelization." Evangelization means spreading the good news of Jesus Christ to those who do not believe. There are three billion such people in the world and the numbers are increasing. But real evangelism does not play the numbers game. Church growth is not of the essence of church mission. Nevertheless, doing evangelism is the one thing that gives meaning to everything else the church must do. It is its raison d'être. There is still the need to focus prime energies of the church to go and tell the good news of God's redeeming love in Jesus Christ to people who have never heard. The world needs it and the church needs to do it. This book will try to make these assertions stick.

We do not want to see the pendulum swing back and forth. We do not want to see the church substitute social works for gospel words, nor the other way around. Evangelization and social responsibility are both integral to the universal mission of the gospel, and we have no right or need to concentrate on one at the expense of the other. The church meets the world with both hands at work, holding out the offer of justifying grace to sinners for Christ's sake, while working tirelessly to do the good works of love for the neighbor's sake. We have received from Christ two things: a Great Commission to tell the gospel and a Great Commandment to love the neighbor. We cannot be obedient to one without the other.

The aim of this book is to recapture the motive for mission in the gospel and to redefine ministry as the means to the end of that mission. Ministry and mission belong together as means to end.

Otherwise the debates about the right ministry within the church become locked into a kind of ecclesiocentric preoccupation with offices and structures. Nothing can be more boring to people inside the church or irrelevant to people outside than to have to listen to endless and fruitless debates about office, ordination, succession, priesthood, episcopacy, papacy, etc., ad nauseam. The greatest threat to the life of the church is the loss of its gospel substance, and the surest way to bring this about is for the ministry to become a bureaucracy functioning to maintain the structures of the organized church, mindless of its subservience to the mission of the gospel to the world.

The trends are obvious in the mainline churches. Bureaucratization leads to secularization. Rigor mortis sets into the body when the heart of the gospel quits pumping blood into the organs of the church. We have seen in recent decades how Western and North American churches have been moving their ministries to the frontlines of action in the service of the kingdom on the left hand of God. They have done a lot of good things, trying to prop up a world that seems bent on self-destruction. At the same time they have retreated around the world from direct evangelistic involvements.

It lies within the nature of the gospel to call people to reach beyond their own tribe, language, culture, class, and borders, to demonstrate in action the catholicity of the church born of the Messiah and his Spirit. Paul went out of his way to evangelize the Greeks; he could have stayed home in Tarsus and carried out local evangelism as James did in Jerusalem. Paul crossed all barriers, and even surrendered the rite of circumcision to make room for Gentiles. The idea of crossing frontiers and breaking down walls of separation is deeply embedded in the gospel. We are not doing holistic mission if we concentrate mainly on people within our own borders, while increasing our global involvements primarily in United Appeal-type humanitarian projects unconnected with the propagation of the gospel.

There is a certain lukewarmness about mission and evangelism in the congregations of the mainline churches. They have been drugged by psychological medicine that has numbed all the nerves in the body except the ones that seek self-satisfaction or self-fulfillment. The narcissism of our age has taken its toll. The fuzziness in theology may be only a symptom of a deeper failure in the life of the church as a whole. The churches in Europe and America are finding themselves in a neopagan situation, so that with evangelism or reevangelization at home proving so formidable a challenge, it is hard to see where the vision and energies will come from to fulfill the Great Commission in more distant places. It would, of course, be foolish to expect that writing another book on theology can perform a miracle. It may only add to the problem. Still, I believe that theology expresses the understanding of faith, and so must do whatever it can as clearly as possible. We need a theology centered in Christ and his cross, placing the mission of the church at the service of the gospel for the sake of the kingdom on its way to the world.

Americans have a new, ugly self-image. American Christians have heard the rising chorus of voices shout, ''Yankee, go home!'' And the missionaries have been coming home. This poses a life-threatening situation for American Christianity. Christianity is healthiest when it strikes the right rhythm between the centrifugal and centripetal motions of the gospel. The best hope for each church is to link its missionary policy to the ecumenical movement. Ecumenism does not exist to place all our ministries in the right order; it exists for mission; it exists to reunite divided Christians ''so that the world might believe.'' When that unity does not exist, the mission is seriously impeded. American churches must become reinvolved in world evangelization through ecumenical means, overcoming their denominationalism. When mission teams become international and multicultural, the loathsome image of the white missionary coming from affluent and powerful Western and American churches will be effectively reduced, and the understandable suspicion of imperialist, neocolonialist, and capitalistic intentions will prove groundless.

The evangelical motives and aims of mission are invariant convictions of a gospel-centered church. This book deals with the bare essentials of a theology of mission and ministry for today's church. The problem of methods has hardly been touched, for the reason that this must be left to the responsible agencies and persons in the fields of mission at home and abroad. Methods are in a sense *adiaphora*; nothing can happen without them, but they vary from age to age and place to place. We are not equipped by the message with a ready-made prescription on how to meet the challenges of our time. All we know is that we must witness to the truth of Christ in the midst of the world religions, or our faith is dead. Dialog may function today as one medium of the essential witness. But we do not propose dialog as an end in itself, but as a means to the end of sharing the truth in love with those who do not yet believe in Jesus and have not been baptized into the community of the new age.

We do not have any sacred instructions that tell us how to encounter a scientific technological culture or how to address the rise of ideologies such as secularism, nationalism, communism, or capitalism. All we know is that Christ alone is the Lord of history and victor over its ruling powers and principalities, and we must tangle with the demonries of our own time and place. We do not have any rulebook on how to carry out the tasks of indigenization, enculturation, and contextualization. All we know is that our Western culture and its accoutrements are not to determine our subject matter, but that our words and deeds are to be signs and tools of a gospel not our own, which neither our blood nor our soil, neither our ethnicity nor our culture, neither our nationality nor our religion, have revealed unto us.

PART ONE:

The Criterion of Mission

1

The Cross as the Criterion of Christianity

The Criterion of the Cross

As a mere theological stripling, just 25 years of age, Martin Luther wrote a letter in which he stated that ''the only theology which was of any value was that which penetrates the kernel of the nut and the germ of the wheat and the marrow of the bone.''[1] At the Heidelberg Disputation of 1518, one year after penning his 95 theses, Luther got to the marrow of the matter. He declared that the only theology of any real value is to be found in the crucified Christ. The essence of a truly Christian theology is what Luther called the *theologia crucis* (theology of the cross), which he sharply distinguished from the more traditional type of theology, the *theologia gloriae* (theology of glory).

Only theology shaped by the cross leads to the true knowledge of the God who is really God. The cross alone is the criterion of the church's identity and its mission to the world. The application of this criterion will disclose what is true and false in the life of the church and its outreach to the world. If the reformation is to continue (*ecclesia semper reformanda*), its thrust must come from a renewal of a cross-centered theology and faith.

Walter von Loewenich has written the definitive monograph on *Luther's Theology of the Cross*.[2] He is joined by other notable scholars—Paul Althaus, Gerhard Ebeling, and Eberhard Jüngel—who support the thesis that from the beginning of his career to the end, the cross of Christ was the distinctive mark of Luther's theology. What is meant by this is not that Luther dwelt on the death of Jesus or the doctrine of the atonement more than on other Christian doctrines. Rather, for Luther the cross provides the criterion of all Christian thought and life; it offers a perspective on all Christian knowledge and shows the way to do theology that is truly Christian. So at Heidelberg in the presence of his fellow Augustinians, Luther said: "That person does not deserve to be called a theologian who looks upon the invisible things of God as though they were clearly perceptible in those things which have actually happened. He deserves to be called a theologian, however, who comprehends the visible and manifest things of God seen through suffering and the cross."[3]

Luther was addressing the question of the nature and method of theology, still a central issue today. Luther was pitting his biblical theology of the cross against the metaphysical speculations of medieval scholasticism. "From this you can see how, ever since the scholastic theology . . . began, the theology of the cross has been abrogated, and everything has been completely turned upside down. . . . A theologian of glory does not recognize, along with the Apostle, the crucified and hidden God alone."[4] In the next breath Luther contrasted the way of the apostle Paul with that of the philosopher Aristotle, whose metaphysics many theologians were following as a valid way to the knowledge of God. Luther did not teach that there was *no* knowledge of God to be found in metaphysical, mystical, and moral approaches, or in other religions. But all of these he labeled as theology of glory, because they all lead up to a glorious God (*Deus gloriosus*), a God who would not be caught dead on the cross of the man in whom there was "no form or comeliness" (Isa. 53:2).

What is so bad about natural theology, speculative metaphysics, or works-righteousness? Why should they and their modern equivalents be ruled out? Simply because they want to deal with *God as*

God, perhaps even very monotheistically and theocentrically. They look away in shame from the God hidden in the suffering and cross of Christ. They want a healthy theology of glory. They want to talk about the power, wisdom, and glory of God, God's works in nature, history, and personality. So they develop uplifting theories by which to ascend to their *Deus gloriosus.*

The theology of the cross works with a completely different criterion and orientation. It seeks to learn of God and to meet God in things that the theology of glory finds to be so much foolishness, powerlessness, humiliation, and suffering. The God who is really God when God is being God for human beings can be encountered and available only in the suffering Christ, and nowhere else. To meet God and to know God in the cross of Christ means that the self must become crucified with Christ; it means that intellectualistic and moralistic pride must be put to death. For God can be known only in the cross and suffering, in the cross of Christ and the cross of the self. The spectators on the hill outside the gate could not see God hidden in the cross and suffering of Jesus. To meet God in the cross of Christ is to die to oneself and to die with Christ.

Such a view, of course, has to do with faith. "God and faith belong together," said Luther. God and faith meet in the suffering and death of Christ. Any other kind of religious experience has nothing at all to do with true Christianity because it has nothing at all to do with the "wisdom of the cross." The theology of the cross is a theology of radical faith, and both cross and faith must be worked into the center of the church's life and mission to the world; otherwise the church indulges itself in cheap worldly imitations and power mongering.

The Identity of God

Luther's theology of the cross is not only a proposal for a new way of doing theology; it entails as well a new concept of God as the crucified God (*Deus crucifixus*). The theology of the cross is a proposal not only for theological method but also for the doctrine of God, for the being and identity of God who is really God, in contrast to the metaphysical approach to the knowledge and being of God. The nature of God and God's attributes were usually defined in advance as a piece of natural theology *remoto Christo* (apart from Christ), and never primarily and exclusively on the basis of God's self-identification with the being of the man Jesus who died on the cross. Even in classical trinitarian theology, God was thought of as the triune God apart from Jesus. God was triune before God became human in the personal life and destiny of the crucified Christ. This means that the incarnation was not thought of as a constitutively self-determining event for the trinitarian being of God. The incarnation was an event external to the eternal life of God. The main sweep of the theological tradition was able to think of God as God without thinking of the crucified Jesus as very God.

This cross-less approach to God gives us a gloriously shame-free way to talk about God. According to Walther von Loewenich, Eberhard Jüngel, and Jürgen Moltmann, Luther reversed this tradition and opened the path to a completely opposite view. This new view is coming into its own only in the 20th century and this is due largely to the initiatives of Karl Barth. In the cross of Christ we find the revelation of the hidden God. To know Christ is to know God hidden in suffering. The hidden God is the crucified God. A speculative theology of glory flees from the hidden and crucified God in favor of an omnipotent God of majesty. Christian faith must speak of no other God than the incarnate God, the human God, the crucified God, because God's humanity is the only means of access to God's divinity. When Luther said that the crucified Jesus is God (*Deus crucifixus*), he did not mean that Jesus can be called God because Jesus' life matches a prior definition of God derived from some other source. We do not already possess the appropriate content for the category of divinity to which Jesus seems to belong. When we say Jesus is God, the subject "Jesus" gives to the predicate "God" its definitive content of meaning. Jesus the crucified Christ sheds light on the identity and meaning of God. There is no other God (*"Es gibt kein andrer Gott!"*). Only by getting things straight about Messiah and message can we begin to make sense about mission and ministry.

Luther put the matter this way in his treatise *On the Councils and the Church*: "We Christians must know that unless God is in the balance and throws his weight as a counterbalance, we shall sink to the bottom of the scale. . . . If it is not true that God died for us, but only a man died, we are lost. But if God's death and God dead lie in the opposite scale, then his side goes down and we go upward like a light and empty pan. Of course, he can also go up again or jump out of his pan. But he could never have sat in the pan unless he had become a man like us, so that it could be said: God dead, God's passion, God's blood, God's death. According to his nature God cannot die, but since God and man are united in one person, it is correct to talk about God's death when that man dies who is one thing or one person with God.''⁵

Luther's words continued to echo in the subsequent tradition in language about the ''death of God.'' It is only because of our lack of acquaintance with the tradition that the contemporary theology of the death of God has been given credit for conceiving something new. In fact, talk about the death of God is not new; it is rooted in Luther's theology of the cross. We hear it again in a Lutheran hymn: ''O great distress! God himself lies dead. On the cross he died, and by doing so he has won for us the realm of heaven.'' Later, Hegel quoted this hymn and gave philosophical expression to the idea of the death of God as an event of the self-negation of God. Nietzsche also picked up the refrain of ''the death of God'' and turned it into a prophecy of coming atheism in modern culture and of churches as tombs of God. But with Hegel and Nietzsche we are moving far away from Luther's theology of the cross.

The contemporary theologian who is carrying out Luther's program of a theology of the cross more consistently than perhaps any other is Eberhard Jüngel, presently systematic theologian at the University of Tübingen.⁶ He is not chiefly a Luther scholar, but an imaginative disciple of Luther in the way he goes about doing theology. He sets forth certain methodological axioms for Christian theology.

1. The meaning of the word *God* is determined for Christian theology by its reference to the person of Jesus. The presupposition here is that God can be known only as God himself speaks his Word to us. For Christian faith Jesus is the Word of God. This is the meaning of revelation.

2. When theology thinks about God in connection with Jesus, it must remember that this man was crucified. Christian theology is fundamentally the theology of the crucified Jesus.

3. From a worldly point of view, there is no necessity to think "God." From the side of human reason or considering the nature of the world there are no necessary grounds for speaking of God. "God is not necessary in a worldly sense; God is groundless in the worldly sense."[7] That spells the death of natural theology, and it gives rise to a theology of revelation in which God is radically free and self-determining in the cross of Jesus Christ.

Jüngel is self-consciously drawing upon Luther's theology of the cross to develop a doctrine of the Trinity. The doctrine of the Trinity originally arose in the context of confessing the man Jesus as true God, but it did not fully take into account the identity of God in the man who died on the cross. It tended to conceive of the death of the crucified one as an event which affected only the "true man" but not the "true God." Classical metaphysics prevented thinking of God as suffering or identifiable with one who died on the cross. Jüngel, taking a cue from Luther's idea of the *Deus crucifixus*, is developing a theology of faith in the crucified one as true God, bringing God's life and Jesus' death into the same frame of reference. Classical Christian theology had such a heavy commitment to Greek metaphysical thought and natural theology that it could not really free itself to think of the crucified one as God. The concept of God's being was so dominated by the thought of absoluteness that the identity of God with the crucified Jesus was never given any ontological status. Jüngel moves from Luther to Hegel to show how the doctrine of the Trinity and the theology of the cross mutually entail each other.

Jürgen Moltmann's book, *The Crucified God*,[8] gives monumental expression to Jüngel's systematic retrieval of Luther's theology of the cross. Moltmann writes: "To take up the theology of the cross today is to go beyond the limits of the doctrine of salvation and to inquire into the revolution needed in the concept of God. Who is God in the cross of the Christ who is abandoned by God?"[9] "The nucleus of everything that Christian theology says about 'God' is to be found in this Christ event. The Christ event on the cross is a

God event. And conversely, the God event takes place on the cross of the risen Christ.''[10] Moltmann also, like Jüngel, assumes Luther's theology of the cross into a quite fully developed doctrine of the Trinity. "The theology of the cross must be the doctrine of the Trinity and the doctrine of the Trinity must be the theology of the cross, because otherwise the human, crucified God cannot be fully perceived.''[11]

Behind these reflections on Luther's theology of the cross lies Dietrich Bonhoeffer's often quoted statement: "God allows himself to be edged out of the world and onto the cross. God is weak and powerless in the world, and that is exactly the way, the only way, in which he can be with us and help us. . . . Only a suffering God can help.''[12] Similarly, a Japanese Luther-scholar, Kazoh Kitamori, wrote his *Theology of the Pain of God* as an interpretation of Luther's theology of the cross in correlation with the Japanese experience of suffering.[13]

There are still other contacts between Luther's theology of the cross and contemporary theology reaching into some very diverse corners. Elie Wiesel in his book *Night* tells about an incident at Auschwitz: The SS hanged two Jewish men and a youth in front of the whole camp. The men died quickly, but the death throes of the youth lasted for half an hour. "Where is God? Where is he?'' someone behind Wiesel asked. As the youth still hung in torment in the noose after a long time, he heard the man call again, "Where is God now?'' And I heard a voice in myself answer: "Where is he? Here he is—he is hanging here on this gallows. . . .''[14] Such an idea is congruent with the Hebraic idea of the passion of God, but it is overruled from the start in Greek metaphysical thought about the nature of God's being.

In Roman Catholic theology, Walter Kasper gives Luther this credit: "Luther's *theologia crucis* first breaks through the whole system of metaphysical theology. He tries consistently to see, not the cross in the light of a philosophical concept of God, but God in the light of the cross. . . . For Luther, the hidden God is the God hidden in the suffering and the cross. We should not try to penetrate the mysteries of God's majesty, but should be content with the God on the cross. We cannot find God except in Christ; anyone who tries to find him outside Christ will find the devil.''[15]

Out of Latin American liberation theology comes Jon Sobrino's book, *Christology at the Crossroads*, in which one of his major theses reads: ''On the cross of Jesus God himself is crucified. The Father suffers the death of the Son and takes upon himself all the pain and suffering of history.[16] Sobrino explains: ''Paradoxical as it may seem, there is a real point to the notion of the 'crucified God'. . . . God himself must be part of the whole process of protest rather than remaining aloof from it. So the question is: Do we find any theological experience where God himself is against God? The answer is yes: the cross. On the cross we find a process within God himself. . . . On the cross of Jesus God was present and at the same time absent.''[17]

The systematic implications of Luther's *theologia crucis* for the doctrine of God are today coming to expression in the works of the new trinitarian theorists, starting with Karl Barth and including theologians like Karl Rahner, Eberhard Jüngel, Wolfhart Pannenberg, Jürgen Moltmann, and Robert W. Jenson. Karl Rahner has formulated the basic thesis of this new trinitarian conceptuality: ''The 'economic' Trinity is the 'immanent' Trinity and the 'immanent' Trinity is the 'economic' Trinity.''[18] This is a rule in trinitarian speculation to which Luther, Hegel, Barth, and Rahner subscribe, despite their wide divergence on other matters. My effort in this section has been to trace this new way of thinking about God in contemporary theology to its chief source in Luther's theology of the cross. A trinitarian basis of the Christian mission can only be as strong as its anchor that lies in a trinitarian theology of the cross.

The Meaning of Existence

Having dealt with Luther's theology of the cross in connection with theological method and the idea of God, we need to ask what it has to do with human existence. It is customary in treating Luther's understanding of the meaning of human existence to turn to his doctrine of justification by faith alone. Justification has been called the ''article by which the church stands and falls'' (*articulus stantis et cadentis ecclesiae*). Theology of the cross and justification by faith alone are linked in the closest possible way. These are not two separate doctrines of theology but two sides of the same coin. The crucified God is the world's justification. Received through faith alone it tips the balance existentially between bondage and freedom. Freedom is the very essence of salvation for Luther. It is at the point of faith's meaning freedom that human existence fits into the scheme of Luther's theology of the cross.

When Luther was a fledgling theologian, some years before 1517, the year of The 95 Theses, he taught the traditional scholastic doctrine of *synteresis* (conscience [lit., "preservation"]), which provides a human point of contact for God's grace.[19] But he finally surrendered that doctrine because it simply could not be made to fit a radical theology of the cross, but instead invites semi-Pelagian rationalism and moralism. In his polemic against Erasmus he argued like a good Augustinian should that there is no *positive* point of contact in the human condition for the working of divine grace. Grace does not find but brings its own point of contact. In light of the cross Luther came to see the radical corruption of human nature and the utter sufficiency of divine grace to deal with sinners apart from the works of the law and the achievements of reason. A theology of the cross proved to be incompatible with a theology of works-righteousness, as well as with a mystical theology that posits a spark of the divine in the human soul, although in his early years Luther was quite fond of some of the medieval mystics. Luther could not find in any of the systems of metaphysics, mysticism, or moralism a rock on which he could build the house of human salvation. His theology of the cross called for new foundations, not merely another structure on the old foundations. Theories about *synteresis*— or any other positive point of contact in human reason, will, or experience—cling to some of the old foundations and work out a system of synergism between divine grace and human potentiality. In his treatise on *The Freedom of a Christian* Luther said: "A Christian is free and independent in every respect, in bondage to no one." At the same time, "A Christian is a dutiful servant in every respect, owing a duty to everyone."[20] That kind of radical freedom to be in bondage to no one and yet a servant of everyone comes, for Luther, from faith in the crucified Christ, and from no other source.

The person who presumes that righteousness can be had in any other way than by receiving the righteousness of God in Christ renders the suffering and cross of Christ useless. "Learn Christ and him crucified. Learn to praise him, and, despairing of yourself, say, 'Lord Jesus, You have my righteousness, just as I am your sin. You have taken upon yourself what you were not and have given to me what I was not." This is called the doctrine of the "happy exchange" (*"fröhliche Wechsel"*).[21]

Faith means freedom because it gets us sinners off the hook of trying to reach the righteousness of God by our own reason and strength. Faith does not justify as some kind of act which a human being can do in the sight of God (*coram deo*), but faith justifies only as pure reception of the gift of righteousness that is from outside (*extra nos*) and not of one's own self. The cross is God's way of shattering the way of works to make way for faith, to "let God be God" and make humans free to live life to the hilt. This courage to abandon oneself fully in freedom is what Luther meant by his audacious word *pecca fortiter* ("sin boldly"); but Luther, of course, added, "believe and rejoice in Christ even more boldly, for he is victorious over sin, death, and the world."[22]

It has been difficult for many contemporary persons to hear Luther's appeal to justification as a gospel-bearing word for our time. The entire Reformation formula, "justification by grace alone through faith alone on account of Christ alone," seems to be enjoying widespread ecumenical consensus at a point in time when it may be least intelligible and thereby virtually noncontroversial. As Karl Rahner puts it so gently: "For a Catholic understanding of the faith there is no reason why the basic concern of Evangelical Christianity as it comes to expression in the three only's should have no place in the Catholic church. Accepted as basic and ultimate formulas of Christianity, they do not have to lead a person out of the Catholic church."[23] Why were Luther's "*solas*" so controversial in his time, both on the right and the left, from Cajetan the Thomist to Erasmus the humanist, whereas in our time they seemingly produce a wide ecumenical yawn? Is it because at last they are being understood, or possibly because they seem so largely irrelevant and allegedly do not deeply speak to the concerns of modern people?

The matter still hovers as an embarrassment over the heads of Lutherans, that at the fourth assembly of the Lutheran World Federation, meeting in Helsinki, Finland, in 1963, Lutheran theologians were delegated to produce a new statement on justification, after many years of studying the issue. No consensus statement came out of the meeting, not because there was not enough time or talent, but simply because Lutherans could not agree that the message of justification meets modern people at the point of their greatest need. So at Helsinki the Lutherans issued a proclamation which stated: "The man of today no longer asks, 'How can I find a gracious God?' He suffers not from God's wrath, but from the impression of his absence; not from sin, but from the meaninglessness of his own existence; he asks not about a gracious God, but whether God really exists."[24] These Lutherans asserted that the question of the modern person is much more radical than Luther's. The question is not: "Does God accept me just the way I am?" The question is rather: "Is there any God at all?"

I still read Karl Barth when I am looking for some good medicine. As though he had an eye on those foolish Lutherans, ten years before the Helsinki debacle, Barth wrote: "Of all the superficial catchwords of our age, surely one of the most superficial is that, whereas 16th-century man was concerned about the grace of God, modern man is much more radically concerned about God himself and as such."[25] The Lutherans took the words right out of Barth's mouth and proved themselves capable of just the kind of superficiality Barth had in mind.

The question of the existential significance of Luther's theology of the cross for modern people should be taken up again. Is it really true that modern people are more profoundly concerned about whether God exists at all than whether God speaks a gracious word for our existence, in our time? Does it really matter to me that God exists if there is no way that I can know whether he cares for me or not? Is that kind of curiosity worth a tinker's damn? Consider the plight of two modern characters, Vladimir and Estragon, in

Samuel Beckett's play, *Waiting for Godot*. These two forlorn persons are standing on a bleak stage of modern life, waiting for someone they call Godot. They have no clear idea about who Godot is, but they deeply sense the meaninglessness of their own existence. By the end of the play they have looked for Godot in vain. If only Godot would come, things would be so different. No longer the empty feeling about life. They blurt out, "We'll hang ourselves tomorrow . . . . Unless Godot comes. And if he comes? Why, then we'll be saved." But Godot doesn't come. The curtain falls upon their despair. Vladimir and Estragon were not famous philosophers, just two modern characters who did not think to separate the question of the existence of God from the existential question of meaning (or salvation) bearing down upon their empty lives.

Or take another example, this from Graham Greene's novel, *The Power and the Glory*. Greene writes about a miserable priest, drunken with whiskey, and the father of a bastard by a village woman. He feels self-condemned; instead of being the saintly priest his people deserve, he lives a sullied and squalid life. Greene's theme in depicting the utter wreckage of human lives is that, if salvation depends on human achievement, there is only damnation in the end. As the priest dies with a drunken belch, he is heard muttering something about forgiveness. In the end, no matter what, there still stands the offer of God's radically objective, unconditional grace hammered out on the cross of Christ for the sake of those who merit only death and damnation.

The Criticism of Society

There is a widespread view that Luther's theology of the cross and the theme of justification by faith alone exhaust their meaning in connection with personal salvation and "the introspective conscience of the West," and that they have little or no bearing on the everyday life of people in the real world. This is a completely mistaken view. The theology of the cross is not restricted to the sphere of subjectivity, but is utterly practical in orienting a person with the right approach to reality. Luther's strongly vertical sense of the divine-human encounter in the cross of Christ most assuredly reaches the horizontal plane of everyday human activity. Luther was not a monk writing a theology for ascetic piety. He broke out of the cloister and led many other religious folk to forsake their vows and venture into the everyday world of practical affairs.

In other words, the cross of Christ and the cross of the Christian cannot be separated. The locus of life under the cross is not in a monastery but in a school, on a farm, in a family, in the everyday secular world. The Christian's life in the world is "life under the cross" and is not confined to the private sphere of religion. The dichotomy between two realms, the religious and the secular, is something that cropped up in later Lutheranism in terms of a dualistic doctrine of the two kingdoms. Luther's theology of the cross and faith alone was not locked up inside the heart of a brooding monk, but erupted into the spheres of society, politics, and secular vocation. The glory of the Christian life in the world is hidden under the signs of suffering, humility, grief, disgrace, despair, and death. "If any man would come after me, let him deny himself and take up his cross, and follow me" (Matt. 16:24). The place to go in following Jesus is not inside the walls of sacred institutions, but outside the gate where he experienced humiliation, forsakenness, and weakness. Such is the life of Christian discipleship; it leads into suffering— not the kind of suffering whereby we work out our salvation by acquiring merits exacted by a righteous God, but the kind of suffering that comes from bearing the cross of Christ, incurring the enmity of the world. The cross-bearing life arouses conflict and strife; Christians ought to expect that they will be regarded as sheep for the slaughter. Martyrdom is not a way of salvation but the price that Christians unavoidably pay in doing hand-to-hand combat with forces of evil in the world. Luther's ethic is one of conformity to Christ, and that means to take the form of the servant in waiting on others.

In the face of violent evil Christ did not repay in kind. Likewise, the only weapons the church as the church of martyrs has are the word and faith. Like Christ himself, the church's strength will be manifest in weakness, humility, suffering, following a course of action that is exactly opposite that of the kingdoms of this world. There is no glory for the church in the present age, for now "we suffer with him in order that we may also be glorified with him'' (Rom. 8:17). This is an eschatological glory that will not be manifest in history.

It has become common to lift up four marks of the church—unity, holiness, catholicity, and apostolicity. Luther placed cross and suffering on the par with these as marks of the true church. From Luther's point of view, a church that wants to be great and glorious in worldly terms, vocal and victorious in political terms, is deeply suspect. There is something wrong with the church when it refuses to accept its suffering condition as essential to its very nature in history.

It is not common to look to Luther for any light and insight on the subject of the Christian life, that is, the sphere of sanctification. Luther allegedly put all his eggs in the justification basket. Nor do many people expect much help from Luther concerning the church's mission in the world. Luther allegedly erected a wall of separation between the church and the world by his doctrine of the two kingdoms. Recent Luther research has established that as surely as these historical caricatures apply to some subsequent forms of Lutheranism, they do not fit Luther.

One of the interesting developments in theology today is inquiry into Luther's theology of the cross for its possible relevance to a critique of society. The Christian lives a total life in different relationships. The Christian lives *coram deo*, that is, in the sight of God. The Christian also inescapably lives in other *coram* relationships:[26] *coram hominibus*, in relationship to other people; *coram meipso*, in relationship to oneself; and *coram mundo*, in relationship to the world. Luther's theology of the cross is fundamentally concerned with the life of a human being *coram deo*. He was, after all, a theologian first and last. But he did not separate his idea of *coram deo* from the other *coram* relationships.

What does the theology of the cross have to do with all these other *coram* relationships? A number of theologians are trying to explore connections between Luther's theology of the cross and contemporary social reality. Jürgen Moltmann, in *The Crucified God*, explores what it means to contemporize the cross in terms of the economic, social, and political situations of modern life. At the time of the Reformation Luther's theology of the cross dealt mainly with the crisis of conscience and the criticism of the church. The question now is: "How can it be realized as a criticism of society?"[27] It is a risky venture, but Moltmann tries to draw the consequence of the theology of the cross for politics. He has made a bare beginning, and he has not come far in spelling out what he means in concrete terms. But what he is trying to do, and I think in the spirit of Martin Luther, is to show that the freedom that flows from faith seeks to widen the range of freedom in the world in political, social, and economic terms. Those who experience the freedom of faith should lead the way in liberation movements that attack situations of exploitation, alienation, and poverty. "Political hermeneutics of faith is not a reduction of the theology of the cross to a political ideology, but an interpretation of it in political discipleship."[28] Moltmann means that the liberation which believers have experienced solely by an act of God should find some real expression in parabolic actions that aim to liberate people from the prisons of class, race, wealth, and ideology. Moltmann's project is to construct a political hermeneutics of the crucified Christ, but when it comes to specifics he tends to fill in the blanks with quite abstract rhetoric tilting left.

The path of a theology of the cross that is critical of society has been carried further by Douglas John Hall in *Lighten Our Darkness: Toward an Indigenous Theology of the Cross.* In constructing his indigenous theology of the cross, he draws on what he calls a "thin tradition" in Christian theology and names as its exemplars Martin Luther, Søren Kierkegaard, and Karl Barth, who are linked together by a theology of the cross. Luther said *"Unum praedica: sapientia crucis"* ("Preach one thing: the wisdom of the cross").[29] Luther's words on his deathbed were: *"Wir sind Bettler; das ist wahr"* ("We are beggars, that's true"). The wisdom of the cross makes us naked beggars *coram deo,* sinners who become rich with the gift of grace and the righteousness of God in Christ.

Douglas John Hall applies Luther's theology of the cross both as "a spirit and a method, a way of conceiving of *the whole* content of the faith and the task of theology."[30] The tricky part in Hall's use of Luther's *theologia crucis* shows itself when he tries to extend it beyond the personal realm of salvation to an ethic of social and

political involvement. Historically the theology of the cross too easily linked itself to an ethic of resignation and quietism. This world
is a vale of suffering; there will always be war, poverty, crime,
greed, and the abuse of power and wealth. That's the way life is;
we must learn to suffer and bear the cross, because there isn't much
we can do to change things. Hall wants to go further than Luther,
and charges: "Luther seemed incapable of developing a social ethic
that could reflect in the structures of society the reforming power
of his gospel. Not only did he fail to explore the potential of his
theology for reforming society, he actually used it *against* social
reform and against those who would have carried it into the political
realm. In the Lutheran world, the theology of the cross became a
way of justifying the powers that be, together with their evils."[31]

Hall sets about to correct Luther in the spirit of Luther himself,
and that is to express the theology of the cross in a social and political
ethic. The starting point for an ethic of the cross is "a real solidarity
with those who suffer."[32] It all begins with the God of the gospel
incarnating himself in human suffering and in the midst of those
who suffer negation.[33] The precondition of the ethic of the cross is
God's own action "in human suffering and degradation, in poverty
and hunger, among the two-thirds who starve, in races that are
brought low, in the experience of failure in exposure to the icy winds
of the nihil, in the midst of hell."[34]

To give some real footing to an ethic of the cross in society, what
is needed, according to Hall, is a new image of the human, a new
imago hominis. What must be crucified and put to death is the image
of the human being as master, as warrior, as destroyer, for the logic
of mastery leads to the death of the human spirit. Just when humanity
is supposed to have conquered the world with science and technol-
ogy, black clouds of death, threatening our whole civilization, loom
up on the horizon. The master race image of humanity led to the
death of millions of Jews in Nazi gas chambers. In communism the
same master image, now shifted to the "people," has produced
dictatorships of the proletariat that have sacrificed millions of dis-
senters on the altars of the coming paradise of the workers. In capitalist countries, our democratic ideals have provided an umbrella

under which mammoth corporations have freely exploited the natural environment.

What Moltmann and Hall have begun in their own way is finding expression in other quarters in promising directions. As we shall demonstrate later, it is this evangelical concept of the cross and not the Marxist idea of praxis that holds great promise as a resource of the theological imagination for social criticism and ethical reflection. When the World Council of Churches at Melbourne, Australia, in 1980, focused on the poor in relation to the kingdom, the theme of the crucified Christ confronting the powers became the key theological concept.[35] When Latin American theologians shift their attention from intellectual alliance with Marxist ideology to the popular religion of the poor,[36] in order to work with the poor to motivate and structure their understanding of their faith and life, they will find their most useful point of contact in a theology of the cross. Perhaps then too they will find in Luther an ally, and therewith feel less the need to impose the rhetoric and slogans of Marxist ideology, which is an ideology made in Europe just as alien to the poor and oppressed peoples of Latin America as any other imported since colonial times.

2

Christ Alone in an Age of Religious Pluralism

The Challenge of Religious Pluralism

Christian theology is currently engaged in a kind of civil war, and the battlefield can be precisely pinpointed in the area of Christology. The occasion for this new struggle is the impact of religious pluralism on the Christian consciousness. The battlelines have been drawn between absolutism and relativism, exclusivism and universalism, Christocentricity and theocentricity, to list just a few of the flag words around which these opponents rally their forces. The clash is between those who stick somehow to the classical focus on the uniqueness of Jesus Christ and those who surrender his centrality so that his place becomes just one among many in the pantheon of the religions. This is the current form of the conflict between a theology of the cross and a theology of glory, with profound implications for the mission of the church.

Religious pluralism is like a bomb that has exploded the Christian consciousness. Even though the early church was born in the midst of religious pluralism, 1600 years of imperial Christendom numbed Christianity into thinking it was the only enlightened, civilized religion with a future in the whole world. Gradually, but with ever-increasing impact, the modern encounter and the scientific study of the world religions awakened theologians from their dogmatic slumbers. For several centuries, dogmatic theology succeeded in protecting the Christian faith from the results of historical criticism. Christianity was the only divine, supernaturally revealed religion, and this could be proved by Scripture, tradition, reason, and common sense. But at the beginning of this century, the laws of historical criticism entered the heart of systematic theology in the person of Ernst Troeltsch, the greatest systematic theologian of the history-of-religious school.

According to Troeltsch, everything that swims in the rivers of history is relative, including Christianity. Everything human is historical and therefore subject to the laws of historical development, including the Bible. Every historical event is interrelated with other historical events, and none can be made an exception by supernatural intervention, not even Jesus Christ. What we have is a universal movement of all the religions on their pilgrim way, and God's revelation in the Bible and through Christ is only a stage in the history of revelation developing in all the religions. According to this iron-clad law of history, there can be no absolute religion; all are relative. There can be no exclusive revelation; and thus no one religion has a right to pass judgment on the others.[1]

All this would mean that there is no essential difference between Christianity and other religions. Christianity is but a relative appearance like all the others. This does not mean that Christianity is not unique; it is unique in its own way, as every other concrete historical religion is unique. None is exactly like the others, just as no human being is exactly like anyone else. It is natural, of course, for people to prefer their own religion, and so it is natural for Christians to believe that Christianity leads the band of all the religions, and to experience salvation in the name of their own savior figure.

The Heritage of Christocentricity

After World War I, Ernst Troeltsch and the theology of the history-of-religions school were quickly superceded by Karl Barth and the dialectical theologians. Troeltsch was viewed as the dead-end of 19th-century Protestantism, marking the end of liberalism. If

Troeltsch wants to study the religions, he then becomes a historian of the religions, and is no longer a systematic theologian of the church and the Christian faith. The Christian theologian does not deal with the religions, so Barth said, but only with the revelation of God. And this revelation is not in human hands, something to be found by studying the phenomena of the religions.

Karl Barth laid down a whole series of new axioms for the next generation of theologians. There is no point of contact between divine revelation and human religion. There is no human faculty that can reach up to God. There is, in fact, no revelation of God outside of Christ, no revelation of God in nature, history, religion, experience, conscience, or anywhere. In fact, many under the spell of Karl Barth, echoing some of the late 19th-century followers of the theology of Albrecht Ritschl, could say, "If I were not a Christian, I would be an atheist."

The whole "death of God" movement in the 1960s can be seen as a radical, albeit a radically degenerate form of Barthianism, because the "God is dead" people still clung to the centrality of Jesus Christ, even though as secular theologians "come of age," claiming to be disciples of Bonhoeffer, they could no longer believe in God or grasp the meaning of God-language.

Karl Barth singled out the Reformation principle of *solus Christus* (Christ alone) as the cornerstone of his whole theological edifice. The history of religions is altogether irrelevant as a source of theology, because of God's sole relevation in Christ. Religions seek to save people, but salvation has all been done once for all in Christ. Because religions try to do what Christ alone can do, they are like towers of Babel that need to be smashed. The big heresy of Christian theology is to look for revelation in the swaddling clothes of religion, or even to look for any point of contact that would prepare for the radical otherness of God's revelation and its absolutely and exclusively unique incarnation in Jesus Christ.

There were no other theologians who stressed the "Christ alone" principle with the same rigor as Karl Barth. Yet, virtually all the great post–World War II theological systems were mounted on the Christocentric principle.

Certainly Rudolf Bultmann and the existentialist theologians claimed with utter clarity that salvation in the New Testament sense is an existential possibility that can *in fact* be realized solely in Jesus Christ, exclusively through proclamation of the Christ-kerygma. For that Bultmann was roundly criticized by Schubert Ogden.[2] The great Lundensians, Gustaf Aulén and Anders Nygren, poured the whole Christian faith into a Christocentric mould. The Christocentric principle was fortified by three levels of theological research going on during the first half of the 20th century. First, there was the renewal of biblical theology, and on its basis the construction of a highly Christocentric theology of the history of salvation which reached its zenith in Oscar Cullmann's *Christ and Time*. Second, there was a new interest in the church fathers, from Irenaeus to Athanasius, and renewed interest in the ecumenical councils, from Nicaea to Chalcedon, which poured new life into the ancient dogma of the incarnation. Third, again all coming to a sort of climax in the 1950s, there was the Luther renaissance, which elevated *"was Luther sagt"* into a self-evident principle. Nothing could be more Christocentric than the picture constructed out of Luther's theology. Of the God who revealed himself in Christ, Luther said, *"Und ist kein andrer Gott"* ("and there is no other God").

These were the great theological movements of the past generation, all working together in different ways to lift high the principle of Christocentricity in theology. Nor was it any different in the theology of Paul Tillich. Tillich always made clear "that the material norm of systematic theology today is the New Being in Jesus as the Christ as our ultimate concern. This norm is the criterion for the use of all the sources of systematic theology."[3]

The Christocentric line in Protestant theology was not, of course, a 20th-century novelty due to Karl Barth. Actually, the main lines coming from Schleiermacher and Hegel, up through Ritschl and Herrmann, never called into question the centrality of Christology in their systems of theology. As soon as Catholic theology entered the modern world of critical historical and theological thinking, it too took over this feature of Christocentricity. The greatest and most influential Catholic theologian in modern times is Karl Rahner, and there can be no doubt that he has operated with a Christocentric standpoint. In fact, his thinking is so Christocentric that, in order to account for the experience of revelation and salvation in other religions, he explains that Christ is actually the final cause of the salvation in all religions, and for this reason people of other faiths may be called "anonymous Christians."[4] As people who do not know Christ, they experience nevertheless a salvation that finally comes only from Christ. It can come from nowhere else. In no other name is there salvation, Christ alone being the mediator between God and humanity.

This Catholic model of Christocentricity has found monumental expression in the Christological works of other leading Catholic theologians, such as Kasper, Küng, and Schillebeeckx,[5] and we could add for good measure the Catholic liberation theologians, such as Gutierrez, Sobrino, and Boff.[6]

In the midst of all kinds of Protestant and Catholic types of Christocentricity, there is a Lutheran model that can still be discerned. Althaus,[7] Elert, Wingren, and others have insisted that the *solus Christus* principle is intended to be primarily a soteriological principle, an immediate correlate of the *sola fides* principle, and must not become the exclusive epistemological principle, the only window of theology, reducing all knowledge of God to God's single final, saving self-revelation in Jesus Christ. It is not a case of all or nothing, all knowledge of God in Christ or nothing at all where Christ is not present through Word and faith. Lutherans have maintained that there is a kind of general revelation of God in the religions, and therefore a kind of natural theology, and they claim Romans 1 as their biblical support in addition to their own experience and knowledge of the human condition and testimonies of people in other religions. Not all experience and knowledge of God can be reduced to the givens of the gospel. That is what it means when Lutherans emphasize the priority of the law over gospel.

This was the "middle way" of Paul Althaus, who stood in the cross fire between Ernst Troeltsch and Karl Barth. A theologian coming from a line of many generations of Lutherans, Paul Althaus steered a middle course between the Scylla of Troeltsch's religious relativism and the Charybdis of Karl Barth's revelational absolutism. He used the principle of Christocentricity, the centrality of God's salvation in Christ, and the uniqueness of the missionary apostolate that drives the church to bring the message of Christ to all the nations.

The Current Attacks on Christocentricity

Tons of missiological literature have been written on the basis of this Christocentric principle, from Kraemer to Hoekendijk,[8] and we could show that this principle has also been the heart pumping blood into the modern ecumenical movement, dominating the themes of all its world assemblies. But things do not stand still in theology. The pendulum swings. There is now under way a broadside blast from many sides against the principle of Christocentricity.

The first attack on the principle of Christocentricity came from H. Richard Niebuhr. In defining Christianity as radical monotheism, he criticized some Christocentric types of theology as a "unitarianism of the second article." Many of Niebuhr's pupils have taken up this attack and have carried it further. Gene TeSelle, in *Christ in Context*,[9] states flat out that Christocentricity is incompatible with the radical monotheism of biblical faith. It makes of Christ a "second God" alongside the one God of Israel. James Gustafson, another of Niebuhr's pupils, has radicalized the attack on Christocentricity, because it pictures God in human terms.[10] It makes faith homocentric and implies that the God who is busy with this vast universe is actually concerned about human needs and human fulfillment. As if God really cares about the salvation of humankind! So Gustafson speaks about *theocentric* ethics, and he demands that the geocentric view of things that a Christocentric theology advances must vanish. Gustafson says, "For theologians, however, the focus of the divine reality remains very much on our planet and on man. This strikes me as odd and wrong."[11] What we are left with in Gustafson's theocentric perspective is a unitarianism of the first article, and no Christology at all, but only a little bit of Jesuology,[12] only a blurry picture of Jesus who models the kind of religious piety that Gustafson believes is most appropriate in a post-Copernican view of the universe.

From England comes an attack on the principle of Christocentricity in a well-publicized book, *The Myth of God Incarnate*.[13] John

Hick launches the attack by calling for a Copernican revolution in theology. This would put God back into the center of the universe of the world religions, and thus dislodge Christ from the central position he has held in the old Ptolemaic scheme of things. Away with the narrow anachronistic parochialism which links the special self-revelation of God and the salvation of humanity to the event of Jesus Christ. Only then will Christianity be able to get on the superhighway of ecumenical openness, theological pluralism, and interreligious dialog.

The British theologians who reject the myth of God's incarnation in his Son Jesus Christ do so for a number of reasons. Their first premise is a definition of the infinity of God, which renders God metaphysically incapable of expressing himself in a definitive way in the one finite particular event of Jesus the Christ. God is God and man is man, and that's that. The finite is not capable of the infinite. *Finitum non capax infiniti.* One of these attackers asks whether the very concept of an incarnate being who is both fully God and fully human is really intelligible. Of course not, because after all, the finite is not capable of the infinite. Another is troubled by the idea of the incarnation, because it is intellectually impossible to make the ontological equation: Jesus equals God. There can be no two superstars in the galaxy of religion: God and Jesus. There can be, they say, no ontologically real incarnation and hypostatic union of God in his personal essence and human nature. Thus the ontological link between God and Jesus is broken. And yet, do not be discouraged, they say, do not lose heart, for as Christians we can still go on chanting our liturgies, saying our prayers, getting our discounts, and doing whatever is necessary to keep the crumbling Church of England going. We can, that is, still go on speaking of Jesus Christ *as if* he were God for us, as long as this is only metaphorical poetry and no longer metaphysical prose.

The person who is now the Paul J. Tillich Professor of Theology at Union Theological Seminary in New York has written *Christ in a Changing World.*[14] He dedicates this book to all who have suffered at the hands of people who claimed to act in the name of Christ. He proceeds to a ''deconstruction'' of the classical Christology on which the church has based its worship, preaching, and mission to the world. One of the favorite slur words of Tom Driver is "chris-tofascism." This term refers to all attempts to place Christ at the center of life and history, and at the center of our personal life as well. Tom Driver calls for a brand new kind of Christology or none at all. His new kind of Christology is one that gets rid of the scandal of particularity. We have no need of a once-for-all Christ in a re-lativistic world. We must absolutely abolish the notion that Jesus Christ is the saving revelation of God that occurs once and once only, once for all time and once for all people. Because of pluralism and relativity, twin lords of modern consciousness, we must dispose of the notion that there is only one Christ for all time, the same yesterday, today, and forevermore. The big mistake of the churches, according to Driver, is to imprison God in the likeness of Jesus. If the relativities of history are to gain a positive meaning, Christ cannot remain "central" or "once for all."

It is this sensitivity to a plurality of cultures, religions, classes, and political systems that mandates that we have a plurality of Christs, a number of evolving Christs increasingly engaged in cross-cultural and ecumenical interaction. The belief that Christ is once for all has produced cultural imperialism in Christian missions, both at home and abroad.

This note of "christofascism" has been sounded by Rosemary Ruether in *Faith and Fratricide*,[15] in the context of Jewish-Christian dialog. In her thesis, the classical Christological tradition bears deep responsibility for the slaughter of Jews in the Holocaust. Christian anti-Semitism allegedly stems from the Christological decisions made by orthodox Christianity in the first five centuries. It was not only Nazis with names like Eichmann who put Jews into the incin-erator; it was Christian belief in Christ as the final Word of God for human salvation that helped to destroy six million Jews. Rosemary Ruether has made the allegation that "anti-Semitism is the left hand of Christology." The historiography of Tom Driver and Rosemary Ruether neglects the fact that those, like Barth and Bonhoeffer and Niemoeller, who opposed the heresy of the "German Christians" did so precisely in the name of Christ the Lord as they rallied around the Barmen Declaration, than which there could be no more Chris-tocentric document in the 20th century.

Not only Protestants, but Roman Catholics are now getting into the act of reaming out the Christocentric core of Christian faith. Paul Knitter is one of the more radical Catholic theologians now questioning the finality and normativity of Christ. Knitter believes that we must remove Christ from the center of God's revelation in order to place Christianity on a par with other religions, and thus make way for an interreligious dialog among equals. Traditional Christology, with its insistence on the finality and normativity of Christ, is not in line with the current affirmation of religious pluralism.[16] We are in the midst of a paradigm shift from Christocentrism to theocentrism, and finally the Copernican revolution in religion and theology will be complete.

Revision of the Christocentric Principle

Is a revision of the Christocentric principle possible in a way that takes full account of the challenge of religious pluralism, and that meets it not only as an external threat, but as a condition internal to the meaning and function of the principle itself? I believe that this is not only possible but essential if Christian faith is to be true to its very origins in an event that contains at its center a vision of eschatological unity for a religiously pluralized world. The event that holds such promise is the resurrection of Jesus of Nazareth as an eschatological event whose inherent meaning created a missionary apostolate that could not be contained within the house of Israel, but sparked a movement that spread like wildfire across the Mediterranean world and beyond to all the Gentiles.

In his last public lecture, in Chicago in 1965, Paul Tillich had a true instinct in calling for a new kind of Christian theology, a theology oriented around the history of religions.[17] He was calling for a return to the fundamental questions of Ernst Troeltsch, all of which had been blown away by Karl Barth. Not the answers of Ernst Troeltsch, but the questions he wrestled with should be taken up again, by way of an understanding of Christianity that locates it within the historical process of the history of religions. That is exactly where Christianity came upon the scene of world history. Tillich called for a Christian theology of the history of religions. One theologian who has given heed to that call is Wolfhart Pannenberg.[18] The future of Christian theology lies on the frontline of the encounter of the world religions, because the future of Christianity itself depends on what happens when it brings the mission of the gospel into the midst of the struggles going on between the religions. Christianity was never meant to be *the* civil religion of the West, of Europe or America. It was never meant to be the exclusively established religion of an Empire or a group of national states.

The gospel is not the private message of ethnic Christians living on sheltered islands. The place for the gospel lies in the historical interaction between the different religions, and not as an ideology to serve the interests of the established churches.

It is the case, of course, that there has been a tremendous increase in the scientific study of the world religions. Departments of religious studies have grown and new ones have sprung up throughout higher education. The labels tell the story: the philosophy of religion, history of religion, psychology of religion, sociology of religion, phenomenology of religion. But in all these departments there is no place yet for a *theology* of religions. There are centers for the study of world religions, like Harvard, but these have not given rise to a theology at the center of the study of world religions. Tillich was calling for a new thing, and Pannenberg has renewed the call for a theology of the history of religions as the horizon within which Christian theology must make its case for the truth of the gospel and the scope of its mission. For the gospel of Christ and his mission belong within the stream of the religious histories of the world.

The Christocentric principle loses its force and meaning when it becomes the private perspective of a closed circle of Christian devotees. This principle is now under heavy attack, an attack that is carried out mainly by an elite class of alienated theologians. What we need now is to take up the call of Paul Tillich and verify the principle of Christocentricity in the process of encountering and interpreting the world religions in their own settings, beginning of course with Judaism—the topic of our next chapter.

The challenge of religious pluralism puts us at the beginning of a new era, one that corresponds very closely to the inauguration of Christianity as a world-historical religion. Christianity began as a messianic movement within the horizon of Judaism, doubly anchored in Jesus' message of the coming kingdom and in the witness of his apostles to his death and resurrection. There are some theologians today who write about Jesus without reference to the resurrection at all and with no eschatological sense of his message. Such is the case with Schubert Ogden and David Griffin,[19] two leading process theologians, who have written books on Christology with no constructive use for the resurrection, producing a complete moralization of his message in the guise of existential rhetoric. This is not the kind of Christology we need in a dialog with the world religions.

We have to go back before we can go forward, back to the most primitive elements of the apostolic *kerygma, didache, leitourgia,* and *paradosis* as they developed on Jewish soil. There is no sense taking Christianity into dialog with the world religions minus its Jewish roots. That only produces the neognosticism that lies at the heart of all these rejections of the Christocentric principle. The first missionaries were all Jews bringing a message ''made in Israel'' to the major cities of the Gentile world. Even the resurrection of Jesus, as Pinchas Lapide argues, was originally a ''Jewish faith experience,''[20] and not something the Gentile world cooked up.

The earliest Christians distinguished themselves from their Jewish brothers and sisters through faith in Jesus as the Messiah. Jews became Christians when they came to believe that Jesus was the Messiah, and the original apostles claimed that the messianic identity of Jesus and the arrival of God's rule and kingdom are bound up with his cross and resurrection. There is no reasonable way to talk about Christianity without centering in on that event.

Those who attack the Christocentric principle also call for the end of Christian mission. What they do not point out is how that simply spells suicide, for there is no Christianity that is not the product of mission. A person cannot be born a Christian. As Franz Rosenzweig, a Jew himself, once said, ''A Jew becomes a Jew by natural birth, but a person can only become a Christian through spiritual rebirth.''[21] It is redundant to speak of ''born-again Christians.'' Every Christian congregation originates through the missionary process. If conversion through mission is at an end, then Christianity itself has come to an end.

3

Jesus among Jews and Gentiles

Introducing the Theological Problem

From the beginning of my theological career I have always been aware of an indispensable, close connection between Christianity and Judaism, Christians and Jews, the church and Israel. No doubt this awareness was originally grounded in the preeminent place given to the biblical canon—both Old and New Testaments—by the Christian community. It was also certainly heightened by studies in the history of theology, particularly the encounter of patristic Christianity with Gnosticism, which tried to de-Judaize the Christian faith. In our century we had the encounter of the Confessing Church with the "Nazi Christians" (*Deutsche Christen*), who similarly threatened to rid Christianity of its Hebrew connections. There never was any doubt in my mind that the church fathers and the Confessing Church were right. In the Christian encounter with other world religions, the Hebrew writings must always hold a unique place as foundation for the New Testament witness, and must never be supplanted by other religious writings in the missionary situation, such as the Upanishads. Nevertheless, this sense of closeness between Christians and Jews has not yet been elevated to the level of a clear and coherent Christian theology of Judaism. It befalls our time to attempt to formulate such a theology in the post-Holocaust situation.

As a Lutheran theologian, I am also aware that I represent a tradition that has had a long history of relations with the Jewish people and, more recently, has been involved in a series of theological dialogs. The Department of Studies of the Lutheran World Federation has published the report of a consultation held in Oslo, entitled "Christian Witness and Jewish People" (1975), and the Division of Theological Studies of the Lutheran Council in the U.S.A. cosponsored a colloquium with the Interreligious Affairs Department of the American Jewish Committee, whose papers are published in a book, *Speaking of God Today: Jews and Lutherans in Conversation* (1974).[1]

The present-day conversations between Lutherans and Jews take place in a new context, conditioned by two major contemporary historical events, the Holocaust and the founding of the State of Israel. We can scarcely exaggerate the impact of these events on either the Jewish or Christian consciousness at work in doing theology today. Some theologians who call for a post-Holocaust theology have been deeply influenced by these world-historical events. Their theological proposals reflect the radicalism which the magnitude of these events demands.[2] In this changed context, many theologians are convinced that all talk of a Christian mission to the Jewish people is out of order. Is this a theologically grounded conviction or a prudentially motivated call for a moratorium?

In the changed context, Lutherans bear a special kind of burden vis-à-vis the Jewish people, because the birthplace of Lutheranism is the graveyard of millions of Jews. Fewer than 30,000 Jews are living in Germany today. No wonder there has been a keen interest among Lutherans to probe as deeply as possible the relations between Christians and Jews.

The Mission to the Jews before the Holocaust

There is no such thing as a uniform Lutheran theology of mission to the Jews. In the 19th century, theologians oscillated between an anti-Semitic and a philo-Semitic approach. Such powerful theological thinkers as Schleiermacher, Hegel, and Harnack regarded Judaism as obsolete. They looked upon Jews as fit candidates for absorption into a modern enlightened religion which they called Christianity. In his dogmatics classic, *The Christian Faith*, Schleiermacher offers this proposition: "Christianity does indeed stand in a special historical connection with Judaism, but so far as concerns its historical existence and its aim, its relations to Judaism and Heathenism are the same."[3] In a similar way Harnack wrote: "To repudiate the Old Testament in the second century was an error, which the great church was right to reject; to retain it in the sixteenth century was a fate from which the Reformation was not able to free itself. But to conserve it since the 19th century as a canonical source is the result of religious paralysis in the church."[4] In Hegel's dialectical interpretation of history, Judaism represents a primitive stage in the history of religions, superceded by Christianity as the absolute religion. In this climate, the mission to the Jews took the form of proselytizing and assimilation by Christian Baptism, the underlying premise being contempt of things Jewish.

In polar opposition to this anti-Semitic approach was that of Lutheran theologians who struggled against the devaluation of the Old Testament in neo-Protestantism. Lutheran theologians like von Hofmann, F. Delitzsch, and C. E. Luthardt supported Jewish missions by a profound love for the Old Testament and deep respect for Jewish people.[5] They accepted a biblical theology of the history of salvation and believed that God's election of Israel has a continuing significance, when its history is viewed from an eschatological perspective. Is such a concern for Israel's vocation in the history of salvation nothing but a more pious form of theological anti-Semitism, as a growing circle of post-Holocaust theologians charge?

As a result of the 19th-century approach to Jewish missions, there was a growth in the number of converts to Christianity. The International Hebrew Christian Alliance (IHCA) was formed. Jewish-Christian communities were formed. This has spurred a controversy over whether the expression *Hebrew Christian* is not a contradiction in terms. As recently as the 1960s the debate over the status of the term *Jewish Christian* was carried on within the Lutheran World Federation.[6] On the one side, Jews who became Christians were struggling to retain their Jewishness. On the other side, some theologians were arguing that being Christian is a third state beyond the division between Jew and Gentile. The upshot, however, is that if the Jewish-Christian minority did not cling to its Jewish heritage, they would inevitably be swallowed up into the dominantly Gentile majority. That would entail a peculiar reversal of Paul's argument that Gentiles need not become Jews in order to become Christians. To pressure Jews to leave behind their Jewishness when they become Christians drives them into a kind of no-man's-land. Yet, theologically, Lutherans have not succeeded in resolving the issue of a Jewish Christianity within the church.

The hard line, represented by Karl H. Rengstorf, holds that Jews cease to be members of their own people when they attain faith in Christ.[7] Countering this view is that of Karl Barth who wrote: "And only a cheerless, unspiritual way of thinking can occasion a Christian Jew to be ashamed of his origin from Israel or a Gentile Christian to hold it against him. It is a mark of supreme indelible honor to be a Christian Jew."[8] The controversy within the Lutheran World Federation in the 1960s was not theologically resolved. Rather, it was decided that further study was needed "of the term 'Jewish Christian' which shall include consideration of its origin, its meaning and its implications for Christians in the State of Israel as well as elsewhere."[9]

It seems to me that the question of missionary outreach being addressed to Christians and Jews today can be answered by Christians only within a comprehensive theology of Judaism that begins at both ends of the spectrum of the history of Christianity. At this end we begin with the sheer fact that some Jews already are Christians. How do we understand the fact that Jewish Christians do exist in the church today? Would it be better that there were not any? Is there something abnormal about it? Abnormal to whom? Is catholic pluralism in Christianity meant to include people from all cultures, nations, races, genders, languages, and classes—all except Jews? Does such a limitation on the meaning and mission of the church in world history make any sense?

The last question drives us to the other end of the spectrum, the origins of Christianity according to the New Testament writings. There we find that Christianity began with a Jew and as a messianic movement within the horizon of Judaism. How do we understand the fact that the first Christians were Jews, and that from their apostolic viewpoint it was entirely "normal" for Jews and Gentiles to become reconciled by a Jewish name? Isn't there something abnormal about the intervening centuries between the two poles when Christianity became almost exclusively Hellenized, and when Jews who became Christians were made to feel unwelcome in the church they founded, or were pressured to shed every trace of their Jewishness?

The cash value of Christian mission or witness among Jews may be that an overly Hellenized church is reaching out for the Jewish roots of its own identity. It may be at least more significant for Christians than for Jews. Some Christians have sensed that placing Jews in an unapproachable class is perhaps a reverse kind of anti-Semitism, and that the loss of the Jewish presence in the church leads to a loss of biblical substance. Again, Gnosticism and nazism are extreme examples of a Christianity with a Hebraic void.

The Ecclesiological Dimension

Terms like *mission, witness, conversion,* and *outreach* are not self-explanatory. Their meaning is linked to the theological context in which they are being used. Today many would abandon all these terms in favor of more neutral terms like *dialog* or *conversation,* on account of so many miserable experiences and horrible memories. At a deeper level we are not quibbling about words, but about an issue that is inescapable from the side of both Jews and Christians. The issue is: How do we understand ourselves as the "people of God"? The church's relation to Judaism is ultimately a theological issue that strikes at the very core of the *ecclesia* and its self-understanding as the covenanted people of God.

Within recent discussions among Lutherans, one meets a variety of views on the relation between the church and Israel.[10] On the one side is the position of radical discontinuity. This is called the theory of displacement: God rejects old Israel, the people of the old covenant, and raises up a new Israel, the people of the new covenant, and this is the Christian church. In the first edition of his book, *Jesus: God and Man,* Wolfhart Pannenberg represented this view.

He wrote: "With the message of the resurrection . . . the foundation of the Jewish religion collapsed. This point must be held fast even today in the discussion with Judaism. One may not be taken in by benevolent subsequent statements of liberal Jews about Jesus as a prophet or allow that the conspiracy for Jesus' death was merely a failure of the Jewish authorities. There may be some truth in such explanations. But the conflict with the law in the background of Jesus' collision with the authorities must remain apparent in all its sharpness: either Jesus had been a blasphemer or the law of the Jews—and with it Judaism itself as a religion—is done away with."[11] Since then Pannenberg has modified his views and has expressed regrets for having reached such an erroneous conclusion, and in fact he has been personally involved in promoting dialog between Christians and Jews on the basis of common ground in the biblical God who is above the law.[12]

On the basis of this either-or position, Jews would no longer be the people of God. There would be only individual Jews, on a par with individual pagans, all to be treated equally as objects of a missionary effort. It is fair to say that some Lutheran theologians, on the basis of a new reading of Romans 9–11, have reconsidered the place of Israel among the nations and now hold a theory of two covenants. Israel is still the people of God; its election has abiding significance. There exists a tragic misunderstanding between these two covenants but, rightly understood, they both retain a significance side by side in the divine scheme of things. There are two ways of relating to the Father, like the "elder and the younger brothers."

A different way of maintaining the ongoing validity of Israel and the church is to affirm the one covenant of God with Israel. Israel is the original people of God, and the church is born of Israel, continuing the original covenant among the Gentiles. Krister Stendahl follows this line. He speaks of Christians as "honorary Jews." He writes: "We need to ask, in spite of it all, whether they are willing to let us become part of their family, a peculiar part to be sure, but even so, relatives who believe themselves to be a peculiar kind of Jews."[13]

The meaning of "mission" or "witness" is vastly altered when we shift from the position of discontinuity to some kind of continuity.

Yet, the issue of continuity versus discontinuity cannot be resolved at the level of comparing Israel and the church. Why mission? Some churches press hard for mission, others back off in favor of dialog. What is at stake? It is necessary to go deeper than ecclesiology to find the place where an answer might be forthcoming.

The Christological Core

Since Jews and Christians share so much common ground, it is important for both communities to try to specify the point at which their paths along the Way diverge. As Lapide says, the dialog between Jews and Christians began as a dialog between the brothers of Jesus and his disciples. Jews are related to Jesus by blood, and Gentiles by water. Franz Rosenzweig says the same thing: "A Christian is made, not born. . . . Christian life begins with rebirth."[14] The basis of the difference between Christian and Jew has to do with the Messiah and the kingdom. This is the core of the issue.

Faith in Jesus as the Messiah is the foundation of the church, and the chief point of difference from the Jewish community. Jesus as Jesus is a bond of union between Jew and Christian; Jesus as Messiah is the point of separation. Many Jews today have reclaimed the Jesus of history as one of their own. "The 187 Hebrew books, research articles, poems, plays, monographs, dissertations, and essays that have been written about Jesus in Hebrew in the last twenty-seven years since the foundation of the state of Israel, justify press reports of a 'Jesus wave' in the present-day literature of the Jewish state. The fact is that much more has been written about Jesus in Hebrew in the last quarter century than in the previous eighteen centuries."[15]

There is some validity to the notion that Jews and Christians are united in Jesus, the man of Nazareth, in spite of being separated by Jesus the Messiah. Jewish scholars have contributed much to our Christian appreciation of the historical Jesus. The works of Josef Klausner, David Flusser, H. J. Schoeps, Schalom Ben Chorin, and Pinchas Lapide have contributed much to our understanding of the Jewishness of Jesus. This bears out one of Martin Buber's insights: "The Jews. . .are 'brothers' of Jesus. . . . Jews know Jesus from within in a way which remains inaccessible to those peoples who acknowledge his lordship."[16]

Jews and Christians may also be united by their common belief in the coming Messiah and the kingdom. Christian identity is marked by belief that Jesus is the Messiah and the bringer of the kingdom of God. Lapide formulates the matter this way: "We Christians and Jews are two types of messianic religions. Said otherwise, redemption is for us the unrelinquishable part of belief. The difference is only in how we preceive this messianism. With you the king stands in the middle, and with us it is the kingdom. With you the redeemer, with us the redemption."[17]

Moltmann reinforces Lapide's observation: "Because Christianity arose out of the belief in the Messiah Jesus and lives in this belief, the original expectation of a messiah in person was pushed into the background in Judaism behind the expectation of a messianic time. And because in Judaism the hope of the Reign of God was dominant, the originally realistic expectation of the Reign of God in Christianity was pushed back behind that salvation which was already brought through Christ. Whoever on the basis of belief in the Messiah Jesus still hoped for that greater Reign was branded as having 'Judaizing tendencies.' Therefore Schalom Ben Chorin was right when he said, 'In general it can be said that while for Judaism the Reign overshadowed the messiah, in the Church Christ overshadowed the Reign.' "[18]

Lapide summarizes their agreement by saying that Christianity is a "Who-religion." It asks: Who is God? Who is the Son of God? Who is the true Messiah? Whereas Judaism is a "What-religion." It asks: What has God done? What is his will? What does he intend for us?[19] A medieval rabbi under interrogation about the Messiah is supposed to have said: "If it is true that the Messiah of which our ancient prophets spoke has already come, then how do you explain the present state of the world?" This is still the question before us. If Christians claim that Jesus is the Messiah, then where is the kingdom? If the kingdom has already come, why doesn't the world shape up?

The question whether the church today has a mission to the Jews must be moved back to the source documents of Christian beginnings. The dialog between Christians and Jews must begin with Jesus of Nazareth, after all preliminaries have broken the ice. The kingdom of God was the central theme in the message of Jesus. Jesus was a ''good Jew'' in relating the coming of the kingdom to the world as the power of God to overthrow the dominion of Satan and to create a new world of lasting righteousness and blessedness. Jesus expected God to establish the power and glory of his reign in the immediate future. Instead, the world has gone on without any real fulfillment for 2000 years. Was not Jesus' expectation of the coming kingdom proved wrong by the ongoing course of history? For when God comes in the power of his rule, the world must change. Things cannot remain as they are. God's coming reign is the power to destroy all resistance to his rule and freely to grant his gracious love to those in desperate need of a new beginning—poor people, tax collectors, and whores. Poor people will become happy, the hungry will be satisfied, and those who weep will laugh. There will be a turnabout of all things when the kingdom comes. And this kingdom is God's kingdom, not a result of human beings becoming more religious and doing good works, nor of military violence or political negotiation. The ethics of Jesus are laden with eschatological presuppositions.

Scholars have debated for decades what Jesus meant by the ''kingdom of God.'' It is now a firmly established result of scholarship that Jesus' person cannot be separated from his kingdom message. His message had aroused hope that God was coming soon in power and glory to put an end to misery, poverty, and oppression—but instead Jesus got caught up in the power struggles of his time that led to his death on the cross. So where was the fulfillment of Jesus' keen expectation of the coming of God and his kingdom to make things right and sinners righteous? It was shattered on the cross. The fulfillment did not come to pass as expected. But after the crucifixion you find a few friends of Jesus interpreting his death and resurrection as a down payment on the kingdom he preached. In this way the person of Jesus became incorporated into his message.

Thus it is not wrong to say that, while Jesus preached the kingdom of God, the apostles preached Jesus Christ. Loisy said it perhaps more cynically: ''Jesus preached the kingdom of God, but what came was the church.''[20] In any case, the claim of the apostolic gospel is that the messianic identity of Jesus and the arrival of God's kingdom are bound up with his cross and resurrection. A corollary of this apostolic claim is that faith is the only mode of access to the salvation which the coming of God with his kingdom has established in the person of the crucified and risen Jesus. This message is called by Paul both "scandal" to Jews and "foolishness" to Greeks, but I feel that it is equally true that it is an embarrassment to Christians. For what is the evidence that the Messiah has already arrived with his kingdom, if the world seems untouched by the good news of its arrival? What sense does it make to say that the victory has already been won, while people are getting killed and we are all perishing. I saw a graffito which said: "More people are now dying than ever died before."

Where is the evidence that the Messiah has already come with his kingdom? Did not Jesus himself promise that, when the kingdom comes, there would be an end to suffering, oppression, poverty, hunger, and death? But world history shows that these bitter realities still continue; they have not been diminished in the slightest degree. Our only answer in face of these facts is the apostolic one: the kingdom is hiddenly present in the person of the Messiah Jesus and the good news of this event can be received only through faith. All efforts to explain this bald proposition are cosmetic in nature. Nevertheless, the early church did acknowledge that in the end the kingdom will also transform the world. But that has obviously *not yet* happened. The arrival of the final kingdom is still outstanding with regard to the world itself. Thus the kingdom is split chronologically into an *already* and a *not yet*. What has already happened is only the first fruits: preliminary, provisional, proleptic. The fulfillment, the parousia, is still to come.

Mission in the Perspective of Eschatology

The truth on which Christianity is based is not dissociable from the living Word and faith. What the Christian message proclaims as true is not a predicate of the world ("It's been getting better and better!") or of the church ("Look at all its glorious success!") or of individual believers ("How deeply spiritual they are!"). Blaise

Pascal knew that faith is a wager. To those who already believe, Christianity may seem as reasonable as Hegel imagined, but Kierkegaard more deeply appreciated the precariousness of faith itself in a not yet finished world.

The eschatological cause of Jesus seemed to end in the failure of the cross. The promises of imminent fulfillment were shattered. Soon thereafter there arose a core of apostles witnessing to the reappearance of the crucified Jesus, which they interpreted as a resurrection occurrence within the framework of Jewish eschatological expectation. The immediate effect of the resurrection encounters was to create an apostolate commissioned to proclaim the message of the power and presence of God's approaching kingdom in the name of Jesus. The office of the apostle is centered in his witness to the resurrection as God's proof that the coming of his kingdom is indissolubly linked to the personal life and history of Jesus. The apostolic mission is not only a reflection of the light of God's eschatological action in Jesus Christ; it is also an instrument bearing God's universal promises to the nations. The eschatological meaning of Jesus is carried forward in the universal mission of the apostles.

The root of Christian identity lies in its apostolicity. Apostolicity means doing the apostolic thing, namely, continuing the cause of Jesus under the conditions of its transformation through the events of Good Friday and Easter, as well as Pentecost and Ascension. There is no other way to retain continuity with the apostles than to keep on doing what they did—going with the gospel, making disciples of all nations, baptizing them in the name of the Father and of the Son and of the Holy Spirit (Matt. 28:19). That is really all that mission means. There is simply no way for Christianity to remain Christian in the apostolic sense without establishing its identity through preaching the gospel of the kingdom in the crucified and risen Messiah Jesus and spreading that witness wherever there are ears to hear. The eschatological message and the apostolic mission together define the being and meaning of the church in history.

The Christian church calls itself not only apostolic but also catholic, bearing in mind the universal scope of the apostolic mission. The mission is universal because of its eschatological character— reaching temporally and spatially in every direction, crossing all frontiers of culture, class, race, religion, age, sex, and whatever else that seems to erect walls of partition and create *apartheid*. Therefore, a church can be apostolic only if it is also catholic, working in line with the universal horizon of the apostolic commission. "Catholic" means going beyond the limits of particularity. This calls for the church to be open in two directions: to the eschatological future of God's kingdom, now already present in the Christ event, and to the whole world in all its splendid diversity. As an eschatological concept "catholicity" points to the movement of the church's universal mission "to the ends of the earth" and "to the close of the age." Then Christ will hand his kingdom over to the Father and God will be all in all.

The form of the apostolate in relation to Jews today may well be the sort of thing that is going on in many quarters, namely, dialog, witness, and conversation. Since a term such as "mission to Jews" carries so many negative connotations, it is well to drop it altogether; it is in any event not a biblical phrase. A similar phrase like "evangelizing the Jews" can also be dropped, because it likewise distorts the essential meaning of the apostolate, and has no New Testament backing. Let us drop these and other such loaded words, which succeed only in conveying the most unfortunate performances in the history of the Christian apostolate. Some evangelical missionary efforts to convert the Jews only recycle a 19th-century approach which forgets what has happened in the meantime. Many people, both Jews and Christians, feel that mission and anti-Semitism are inextricably associated. So where do we stand today?

Many Christians today wish to exchange the former approach of missionary zeal for one of faithful witness in the context of dialog and ministry in the form of service to Jewish people according to *their* needs. What is essential is that the Christian community retain the meaning of the apostolate as an eschatological reality in history, and this means "being sent" also to witness and serve with a message of reconciliation for all humankind, including Jews.

In Rom. 11:17-18 Paul says, "But if some of the branches were broken off, and you, a wild olive shoot, were grafted in their place to share the richness of the olive tree, do not boast over the branches. If you do boast, remember it is not you that support the root, but the root that supports you." The dialog between Jews and Christians must get down to the roots and in that sense become truly "radical," because both sides have been boasting about their branches, that is, the sorry ramifications of their conflictual histories. The question, "Who is Jesus of Nazareth?" forces both sides to go to the roots of Judaism and of Christian beginnings. We will then deal again with the meaning of such terms as Messiah, kingdom, atonement, and resurrection, all of which grew up on Jewish soil and are simultaneously root concepts of Christian identity. Today, perhaps for the first time since the first century, we are in the position to hold such a dialog. In such a real dialog we can well imagine the possibility that sensitive persons will actually convert to the witness of the other side.

I agree with a statement made by Franz Rosenzweig: "Christianity, as the eternal way, has to spread ever further. Merely to preserve its status would mean for it renouncing its eternity and therewith death. Christianity must proselytize. This is just as essential to it as self-preservation through shutting the pure spring of blood off from foreign admixture is to the eternal people. Indeed proselytizing is the veritable form of its self-preservation for Christianity. It propogates by spreading."[21] I would add only this: This is equally true of other living religions. Today we have Christians converting to Hinduism, Catholics to the Moonie movement, Lutherans to neopaganism, and Jews to Christianity. When it happens, it happens, and all the slick deprogramming techniques will not succeed in deconverting people back to their former belief. As Christianity continues to lose its privileged position in the marketplace of the competing world religions, it will more closely approximate the New Testament situation. We will be driven back to the basics of *kerygma, didache, leitourgia, paradosis,* and *diakonia.*[22]

PART TWO:
The Horizon of Mission

4

Toward a Holistic Theology of Mission and Evangelism

The Biblical Basis of Mission

The contemporary church in all its branches is profoundly engaged but seriously divided on the theology and practice of mission and evangelism. There are roughly three blocs: the ecumenicals, the evangelicals, and the Roman Catholics. There is some overlapping, but these three groups are organized worldwide along different lines of authority. Then there are Lutherans. Where do they fit? They have a strong affinity in some ways with each of these, but are not completely comfortable with any. Lutheranism is primarily a confessional movement of international scope that should feel free to share its witness to the gospel with all other groups of Christians who confess Jesus Christ as Lord and Savior in accordance with the Scriptures.

Churches today are in search of a theology of mission and evangelism as never before because they are going through a period of transition in which one chapter of church history is drawing to a close, and the outline for the next chapter is as yet unclear. The frequent conferences and consultations on mission in all major blocs—Bangkok, Lausanne, Puebla, Melbourne, Pattaya, Stavanger, etc.—are a healthy sign of the general awareness that the future of the Christian mission is being molded in the struggles of the present time. The search for a biblically based, evangelically motivated, ecumenically oriented, and practically grounded theology of mission and evangelism on the threshold of the next millennium is continuing. This chapter is a modest contribution in the same direction from a Lutheran perspective.

When churches are involved in a great dispute, it is important they they resolve their differences on the ground of their shared identity. A theology of mission and evangelism that is binding on all Christian communities must begin with the foundations of their common Christian faith and calling. The mission of the church and its evangelistic task are not options which churches may choose when the weather permits. From a worldly point of view there is never an appropriate occasion for the church's witness in words and deeds. From the church's point of view, mission and evangelism are a reflex action of the voice of the risen Lord who placed the church in motion, charging it to proclaim the gospel to the ends of the earth to the close of the age.

We should be clear that when we speak of mission and evangelism, we are not speaking of some variables that might belong to this or that model of the church constructed by the theological imagination. Mission and evangelism are invariable structures of the church, firmly embedded in the apostolic traditions of our Lord's final summons to his disciples. We find the missionary charter of the church in the four Gospels and in the Acts of the Apostles, formulated in somewhat different terms. In Matthew the risen Jesus appeared to his disciples and said, "Go. . . make disciples. . .baptize. . . and teach" (Matt. 28:19-20). In Mark he said to the disciples, "Go into all the world and preach the gospel to the whole creation" (Mark 16:15). In Luke he said to them, ". . .repentance and forgiveness of sins should be preached in his [Christ's] name to all nations, beginning from Jerusalem" (Luke 24:47). In John the risen Jesus appeared to his disciples and said, "As the Father has sent me, even so I send you" (John 20:21). Then, in the Acts of the Apostles, Jesus presented himself alive after his death and spoke of the kingdom of God and said, "You shall be my witnesses in Jerusalem and in all Judea and Samaria and to the end of the earth" (Acts 1:8).

The apostolic pattern of *going* into the world follows that of the incarnation of the Son of God. John's gospel gave it classical form: "As the Father has sent me, even so I send you" (John 20:21). Advance signs of this model of "sending and going" can be seen in God's election of his people Israel. God called and sent Abraham, commanding him to go from his home country into a place and a future unknown. God sent Joseph into Egypt, he sent Moses on a mission to liberate Israel, and he sent a long line of prophets to declare his promises to the people. Finally, at the right time "God sent forth his Son" (Gal. 4:4). And, on the day of Pentecost, the Son sent forth the Spirit.

Mission was involved in the very nature of the gospel that Paul carried to the Gentiles. The "mystery" of God's righteousness, the "secret and wisdom of God" concerning the salvation of the world, has now become disclosed in Jesus Christ (Rom. 1:17; 1 Cor. 2:7). This is the good news that must be "made known to all nations" (Rom. 16:25). How? Through the ongoing proclamation of those who have themselves heard and believed the gospel of God's deeds in the history of Israel and in the life, death, and resurrection of Jesus Christ. "Faith comes from what is heard," said Paul, "and how are [people] to believe in him of whom they have never heard? And how are they to hear without a preacher?" (Rom. 10:14,17). All believers are preachers in the sense of bearing witness to the full and final revelation of the world's reconciliation through Jesus Christ our Lord.

Conflicts over Mission and Evangelism

In light of such clear biblical imperatives for mission, it seems somewhat surprising that there should be so much confusion in the contemporary church. Confusion began to arise when the concept of mission suffered a great inflation. Stephen Neill stated that, when mission comes to mean everything the churches do, it ends by meaning nothing at all. Mission becomes everything the church might do in relation to the whole world, and all these things are embraced by the term "holistic mission." Instead of being a term which unites evangelicals and ecumenicals, it has become a bone of contention, each side claiming to be "more holistic than thou." Evangelicals fear that when mission is defined in terms of humanization, development, and liberation, or as a program to combat racism, concern for industrial relations, economic development, and agrarian reform, the classical meaning of mission as primarily evangelism gets lost in the shuffle. The church then finds itself mostly preoccupied with projects around the world at which it can be only second best, while devoting a decreasing percentage of its total resources in personnel and material to what she alone as the church, and what no other agency in the world, can do.

Let us try to focus on the real controversy. The controversy is not only between ecumenicals and evangelicals. It regularly breaks out at every world conference on evangelism—e.g., Lausanne, Melbourne, Pattaya, Puebla, and Stavanger (LWF).

First, we should try to be clear about what the controversy is not. The controversy is not over whether the church should be involved in efforts to promote justice, alleviate hunger, overcome the uneven distribution of wealth, attack ignorance and superstition, stand in solidarity with victims of oppression, negotiate peace between tribes and nations, assist economically underdeveloped peoples, in short, create a better world order in which justice and peace prevail. The controversy does not lie here, because people on every side of the issue profess to be in favor of a general improvement of living conditions for all who inhabit planet earth. All of these causes can be seen within the horizon of the concern of the whole church for the whole world in all its dimensions. For the church lives in a world which belongs to God from its original point of creation to its final point of consummation, according to the biblical vision of things.

Where, then, does the controversy lie? The evangelicals have spoken in a steady stream of publications from Lausanne to Pattaya and beyond. Their chief concern is to retain what they call the classical view of mission, based on the Bible. They define the classical biblical way of regarding mission as "carrying the gospel across cultural boundaries to those who owe no allegiance to Jesus Christ, and encouraging them to accept Him as Lord and Savior and to become responsible members of His church, working, as the Holy Spirit leads, at both evangelism and justice, at making God's will done on earth as it is done in heaven."[1] According to these evangelicals, mission can include a lot of things, such as education, literacy programs, agriculture, medicine, dialog, and social action, provided that their purpose is so to witness to Christ that people might believe in him and become members of his church.[2]

Evangelicals construct a framework of *doctrines* to uphold their picture of mission.[3] These doctrines are so familiar, we need only mention them: (1) the absolute inspiration and authority of the Bible; (2) the immortality of the soul and everlasting life for believers in Christ; (3) the sinfulness of humanity and the need of personal conversion; (4) Jesus Christ as the only Mediator between God and the human race; (5) the church as the body of Christ and the central agent in God's plan of redemption; (6) the evangelization of the world, to be completed before the end of the world and the return of Christ; (7) the primary mission of the church to evangelize the world and bring about the growth of the church; (8) the whole missionary movement as under the direction of the Holy Spirit.

These doctrines seem to offer a cool summary of the evangelical faith. But when turned against the ecumenical theology of mission they start shooting fire. The evangelicals' indictment of the ecumenical conciliar theology of mission is based on their perception of its leading characteristics, which can be summarized as follows:[4] (1) The mission of the church concerns everything that God is seeking to do in the world, for the world and not the church is the object of God's mission. Therefore liberation and revolutionary movements going on in the world are aspects of the *missio dei*, and the church is called to participate in them, perhaps even to be in the vanguard. (2) God is at work to bring in his kingdom of peace and justice, and the church as a light among the nations must act prophetically to attack all forms of imperialism and totalitarianism. (3) God is at work in all the religions of the world, and the church must enter into dialog with them as a partner among equals, and thus learn what they have to contribute to the wisdom of the world and the salvation of humanity. (4) The essence of evangelism is concerned with changing the evil structures of society so that God's will may be done. This means that it is more important for the church to address itself to breaking down unjust social structures than to aim for the conversion of individuals. (5) Since the church is essentially one, it is wrong to convert Christians from one denomination to another, even if their connection with a particular church is of the most nominal kind. For the sake of ecumenism all such activities are decried as proselytism. (6) The church is, of course, to preach *salvation today* (Bangkok), but this salvation means to free people to become fully human (humanization) by lifting their economic, social, and political burdens and breaking down obstacles having to do with race, creed, color, or class. (7) Conversion should not be narrowly conceived in religious terms as switching systems of belief and practice, but rather in terms of turning toward things that embrace a more abundant life for all, such as basic human rights, freedom of thought and speech, participatory democracy, tolerance of other religions, etc. (8) Churches must accept social responsibility, engage in mutual help, assist those in need, improve the lot of children and women, fight racism, etc. For the conciliar theology of mission, social justice is the supreme task of the church rather than to proclaim Christ as the only Savior of humankind. (9) The ecumenical missiology uses many of the old words but means something totally different by them. Although evangelicals hear the ecumenical statements using the same key words from Scripture and tradition, they charge that two radically different systems of doctrine are battling for acceptance. (10) Another ecumenical axiom the evangelicals repudiate is that all the evangelism to be carried out in any country is to be done by the local national churches. The era when Christians of one land went to evangelize non-Christians in another has come to an end. This is permissible only when a local national church requests missionaries from another country, otherwise there is danger of foreign control—shades of colonialism and imperialism.

Leaders of the ecumenical movement would protest that this is not a fair characterization, but a caricature, putting the worst construction on the ecumenical pronouncements. But there are evangelicals within the ecumenical movement who believe there is some truth to the charges. John Stott, an Anglican evangelical, stated at

Nairobi, "It seems to many of us that evangelism has now become eclipsed by the quest for social and political liberation. . . . We question whether the WCC has any longer a heartfelt commitment to world evangelization."[5] Stott and others claim that the official ecumenical theology of mission pays lip service to evangelism in the classical sense; it is never so undiplomatic as to repudiate it, but basically moves ahead to give most time, money, and staff to promote substitutes for classical evangelism, such as relieving poverty, racial discrimination, injustice, and oppression, and worst of all, replacing proclamation with dialog.

In stark contrast to their deprecatory attitude toward the ecumenical conciliar theology of mission and evangelism, evangelicals give the latest Roman Catholic theology of mission very high marks. Vatican II promulgated the authoritative theology of mission in *Ad gentes* ("The Decree on the Missionary Activity of the Church"). About this official document one evangelical has written: "It clearly sets forth a high biblical view of what Christian mission ought to be. A great deal of the confusion in mission today would be cleared up if the honest way in which *Ad gentes* handles what the whole Scripture has to say in regard to mission were to be widely copied."[6] Evangelicals like its biblical doctrinal content. "It expresses a view of God, Christ, humanity, sin, and salvation which necessitates discipling the nations. . . . The missionary task of the church set forth by Vatican II is clearly that described in the Bible."[7] They like its clear statement that the human race needs salvation from sin, that God has acted to save all human beings through faith in Christ and life in his body, the church, that Christ has commissioned his followers to disciple all peoples of the earth, and that finally there is eternal life for the redeemed. It is clear that evangelicals find powerful reinforcement for their convictions about mission and evangelism from the official documents of the Roman Catholic church.

It is perhaps worth noting that while Lutherans have held a celebrated, if not privileged, position in the bilateral dialogs with Roman Catholics, all of their dialogs deal with intraecclesial topics of a traditional sort and have little or no bearing on the burning issues of mission and evangelism in today's world. Here the evangelicals have gotten more quickly to the point with Roman Catholics than have Lutherans. The irony is that supposedly the chief motivation behind the ecumenical drive toward the unity of the church is for the sake of mission—"that the world might believe." But this note "that the world might believe"—has been virtually absent from the many rounds of dialogs between Lutherans and Roman Catholics. It is more than irony; it is tragedy. For it places the dialogs under the shadow of a backward-looking, past-oriented hermeneutic of inquiry. After all of the agreements have been added up, what difference do they make? For whose sake do they exist? Now we are informed that the next round of dialogs will deal with Mary and the cult of the saints. *Cui bono?*

However, Roman Catholicism is not only its official voice. There are unofficial voices within the Roman Catholic church that take quite a different line from the official pronouncements of the teaching authority, the magisterium. These other voices come predominantly from the circle of liberation theologies. They move in quite a different direction, more in sync with the ecumenical theology of mission. For this reason, when officials of the ecumenical hierarchy invite Roman Catholics into their consultations, they generally call upon representatives of the liberationist perspective, rather than of the official magisterial theology. Ecumenism becomes easier when we pursue the policy of selective ecumenism.

Liberation theologies do speak, like the ecumenicals, about the good news of the gospel concerning political and social liberation. They are concerned more for orthopraxy than orthodoxy. They are equally concerned about changing social structures and overcoming systemic forces of evil. Their chief focus of concern is also the "poor and the oppressed." From the point of view of a theology of mission and evangelism, the evangelicals obviously have the same difficulty with the newer liberation theology of mission as they do with the ecumenical theology of mission.

Among Roman Catholics, however, even more radical views on missiology can be found. At Maryknoll, New York, in 1981, some Catholic theologians were assembled to develop a "new missiology for the church."[8] They were asked to outline a whole new approach to mission, one that could serve—God forbid!—for decades to come.

Their first premise was that the traditional Christian approach, Catholic as well as Protestant, of trying to convert persons who do not believe in Christ and of establishing the church is quite inadequate. We are told they spelled this out to their mutual satisfaction. Their new premise was that proclamation today is most effective when it takes the form of dialog, thus drastically relativizing the common notion about the universal need of salvation through Christ alone. Rather, the faiths of other peoples must be reverenced; Christ is only a symbol of what God is doing in a plurality of religions. The starting point of this new missiology is the option for the poor in today's world. The basic goal of mission, they said, is "to promote and serve the unification and healing of our divided, wounded humanity through bearing the burdens of all and through sharing resources, with full respect for humanity's invincible cultural pluralism."[9] This will radically change the way missionaries behave and even who is to be considered a missionary (an understatement!). Missionaries who go out will discover the seeds of the kingdom already there at work, and all they will ask is to participate in its growth among different peoples and cultures.

No one is asking Lutherans to arbitrate this worldwide conflict over evangelism between evangelicals and ecumenicals. Actually, the conflict is rather onesided; whereas the evangelicals are on the attack, for the most part the ecumenicals are not returning the fire. If evangelicals would enter the World Council of Churches, they would bring their gifts to bear on the internal discussions of the ecumenical movement. However, even so, the evangelical critiques are not being ignored. I think it might be fair to say that the most recent ecumenical document coming out of the Commission on World Mission and Evangelism (CWME), entitled *Mission and Evangelism—An Ecumenical Affirmation,* manifests the kind of evangelical focus and clarity that should surely blunt the sometimes fierce attacks by the evangelicals. This document excels in the use of very biblical, Christ-and-gospel-centered language and imagery. I read it as a swing of the pendulum in the right direction. The soundest evangelical convictions are incorporated into this newest ecumenical affirmation and should serve to correct the widely perceived secularizing tendencies that have also circulated in some ecumenical documents. If the evangelicals had not made such a fuss and set up rival international congresses, this new document would probably not have achieved such explicit continuity with the classical convictions on the topics of mission and evangelism.

Perhaps in the next decade we might expect greater convergence between the two main approaches. For, as the ecumenicals have made a move to embrace the evangelical concerns, the evangelicals are likewise making moves from the other side to accommodate the ecumenical concerns. A growing number of evangelicals call for greater social responsibility and striving for justice within the scope of mission and evangelism.[10] They too have come to see the limitations of a soul-winning personal style of evangelism and church-planting that leaves out of account the total context in which people live. There are tensions among the evangelicals just as there are among ecumenicals.

Distinctive Lutheran Emphases

Where do Lutherans stand in this field of tension? Are they too ecumenical for the evangelicals and too evangelical to be at home among the ecumenicals? Do Lutherans represent a *via media*? Is it even necessary to reach a distinctively Lutheran position on mission and evangelism? May it be that Lutherans can rejoice over the rapprochement that may be now occurring, as both ecumenicals and evangelicals respond to criticisms calling for corrections within their own ranks? Is there really that much difference between the Lausanne Covenant and the new Ecumenical Affirmation on Mission and Evangelism?

Yet, Lutherans have a way of wanting to put matters in the light of their own confessional principles.[11] They have their own roots of origin and ambiguous development.

Lutheranism was not a product of the modern missionary movement. It began as a confessing movement within Christendom for the sake of renewing the church by the pure word of the gospel. This accounts for the fact that Luther and the other reformers gave very little attention to the movement of the gospel to non-Christians beyond the pale of Christendom. Nevertheless, Luther clearly recognized that the same gospel which reforms the church must traverse the whole world. He said: "It is necessary always to proceed to those to whom no preaching has been done." [12] The same view of the universal scope of the gospel is clearly expressed in the Lutheran Confessions. In the Large Catechism we read this explanation of the Christian's daily prayer for the coming of the kingdom: "This we ask, both in order that we who have accepted it may remain faithful and grow daily in it and in order that it may gain recognition and followers among other people and advance with power throughout the world. So we pray that led by the Holy Spirit, many may come into the kingdom of grace and become partakers of salvation, so that we may all remain together eternally in this kingdom which has now made its appearance among us." [13] In a summary statement the explanation concludes: "All this is simply to say 'Dear Father, we pray Thee, give us thy Word, that the gospel may be sincerely preached throughout the world." [14]

Whereas Luther recognized that the preaching of the gospel throughout the world is still going on, some of his most zealous followers in the period of orthodoxy taught that the era of missions ended with the death of the apostles, with their having fulfilled the command of Christ to take the gospel to the world. The heathen of today will be deservedly punished for their fathers' refusal of the gospel. [15]

The modern debate over the future of the Christian mission to non-Christians, still going on as intensely as ever, began when Lutheran pietists challenged the prevalent notion that Christ is for Christendom. Ever since then Lutheranism has played a major role in the new period of church history inaugurated when Western Christians, both Catholic and Protestant, sent out missionaries and planted new churches in farthest lands. In the 19th century, Lutheran missionary societies from Germany, the Scandinavian countries, and America competed with other Christian groups in an effort to start new churches true to the confessional teachings of their respective mother churches. This was a pre-ecumenical phase of the modern world missionary movement. Established Lutheran churches wanted their offspring to be true to the Lutheran Confessions, as true tests whether they were rightly communicating the gospel through word and sacraments.

Wherever Lutherans have been active in mission and evangelism around the world, they have imprinted the confessional marks of their identity. Lutherans representing young churches from Africa and Asia have learned to speak the same confessional language, and frequently testify in ecumenical circles to the value of their distinctively Lutheran heritage. In an effort to formulate an authentically Christian theology of mission according to our confessional interpretation of Scripture, Lutherans agree on certain of its essential elements.

The principle of *grace alone* makes clear the unconditional nature of God's declared love in Jesus Christ. The church's mission does not stem from her own initiative, but has its sole source in God's freedom to act graciously in behalf of humanity.

The principle of justification by *faith alone* affirms that human beings cannot achieve the righteousness God requires through any kind of religious rites, moral actions, or sacrificial service. No prior conditions may be laid down as prerequisite to receiving gratis the good news of the gospel.

The principle of *Christ alone* means that God's unique self-identification with the person of Jesus Christ is the sole criterion of saving revelation in history, and that there is no need of another mediator between God and humanity.

The principle of *Scripture alone* means that the church's message to the nations will always be judged by the definitive witness of the Scriptures to the final revelation of God in Christ.

The *confessional principle* provides a proper understanding of the relationship between Scripture and tradition, giving Lutherans a positive attitude toward later developments in the life of the universal church in matters of liturgy, doctrine, and polity, provided these things do not obscure the purity of the gospel.

The principle of *Word and sacraments* holds that for the unity of the church it is sufficient to agree on the essentials of the gospel, and that all other traditions, however ancient or memorable, must not be imposed as ecumenical obstacles.

The *law/gospel* principle preserves the preaching of the church from confusing the biblical gospel with philosophy, ideology, or other systems of salvation. The principle works as a prevention against syncretism.

The principle of the *priesthood of all believers* means that every Christian has received the free gift of grace through Baptism and has been commissioned to spread the good news of the gospel.

The principle of *faith active in love* means that believers in Christ have been set free for a life of humble service, to obey both the Great Commission in words of witness and the Great Commandment in works of love.

The *two kingdoms* principle means that the church acknowledges God's two ways of working in the world, through the general history of culture, morality, and religion, on the one hand, and through the special history of salvation culminating in the gospel of Jesus Christ, on the other hand.

When these distinctively Lutheran principles are applied to a theology of mission, they define the church's self-understanding and determine the priorities on its agenda. God created the church to serve the world by carrying the good news of his kingdom in Jesus Christ to all the nations. This is a task unique to the church; no other institution can do this one thing needful. It is therefore imperative that the church now as ever before apply its major effort to that task which the church alone can do, while also working in partnership with all others who seek justice and the promotion of human welfare.

Essential Elements of a Theology of Mission

We will offer only a bare sketch of the essentials of a comprehensive theology of mission from a Lutheran perspective that will serve to embrace the legitimate motifs developed in the three main ecclesial blocs of thought on this subject—the ecumenical conciliar, the conservative evangelical, and the Roman Catholic. It is clear that Lutherans must go beneath their own confessional criteria to the scriptural foundations common to all parts of the church.

The idea of the kingdom of God has been a dominant strain in missiological thought since the 19th century. The eschatological perspective continues to hold its own today under the impact of critical studies focusing on the preeminent place of the kingdom of God in the message of Jesus. The conservative evangelicals have consistently viewed the kingdom in otherworldly furturist terms, whereas the ecumenical liberationist theology stresses the this-worldly, here-and-now dimensions of the kingdom at work in history. A thoroughgoing proposal to take up the idea of the kingdom of God as the starting point for a theology of mission and evangelism will necessarily embrace both the otherworldly, future-oriented and the this-worldly, present-oriented concerns.

The danger on the evangelical side is in detaching the kingdom of God from the actual events of world history and relating it almost exclusively to individuals and the salvation of their souls in a world beyond. These elements need not be jettisoned. Taken in their one-sidedness they narrow the scope of biblical hope for the coming kingdom. The danger on the other side is the revival of the liberal doctrine of progress, which equates the kingdom's *coming* with the world's *becoming,* whether in terms of dialectical process, evolutionary progress or revolutionary praxis. The kingdom of God is *God's* and cannot be planned and built up by the religious and cultural works of humankind.

The purpose of the church's mission is to invite people to accept the promised future of God through a hope grounded in Christ. The shape of this future and hope comes from the history of God's promises inaugurated by the election of his people Israel, ratified by the life, death, and resurrection of Jesus Christ, and propagated by the apostolic kerygma. These promises are incarnationally grounded in the kingdom of God that has already arrived in the hidden power and glory of God's gracious presence in the cross and resurrection of Jesus. Theology of evangelism must always be formulated in light of the promise and the future that broke through the history that runs forward from God's election of Israel to the resurrection of Jesus and his sending of the Spirit.

The church today must be normed by what is apostolic. Continuity with the apostles means to be fired by the original eschatological drive of the early Christian apostolate and to follow the trajectory of its world missionary outreach. Primitive Christianity taught that the church is an eschatological *koinonia* that already has a share of the final fulfillment of the kingdom in Christ through faith in the Word and life in the power of the Spirit. The core of apostolicity is the witness of the apostles to the crucified and risen Jesus. The office of the apostles is centered in their witness to the resurrection of Jesus as God's proof that the coming of his kingdom is inseparably linked to the name of Jesus. Hence, there can be no other gospel and no other name, as far as the apostolic church is concerned. Any church that does not bear this mark of apostolicity is pseudochurch, a Judas-church.

Contemporary theology has adopted the word *prolepsis* to try to manage this idea of the realized future in the present time of Jesus, which is now past to us but without ceasing to be still our outstanding future hope. The church exists *from* the kingdom of God which Jesus proclaimed and embodied in his own person and ministry; and it exists *for* the world for which Jesus died and was raised again. The kingdom of God toward which the church is striving in its missionary obedience embraces the future of the whole world. The church is sent into the world to invite persons to participate in the kingdom through faith in Christ and membership in his community. It is this special relationship of the community to the kingdom in Christ that determines the core of its exclusive mission to the world. This exclusiveness does not translate into triumphalism or arrogance, because the church is on the way, its mission is underway, the way of life under the cross.

In light of this trialog—kingdom, church, and world—we can see in church history and in the present three possible ways to distort the mission of the church. The first is to reduce the church's mission to the kingdom of God, in terms of an apocalyptic otherworldliness that leaves the world behind. The second is to reduce the church to itself, in terms of an identification of the kingdom with the church, treating the world only as raw material for church growth. The third is to reduce the church to the world, in terms of secularizing the church, its message and mission, in conformity with what the luminaries of the world define as avant-garde. The three blocs we dealt with earlier in this chapter betray characteristic tendencies that conform to these three types of reductionism, the evangelicals to eschatological otherworldliness, Roman Catholics to hierarchical church-centeredness, and the ecumenicals to secularizing world-conformism.

A Lutheran theology of mission and evangelism must take seriously Luther's *theologia crucis* in every aspect of its policy and program. The ecumenical movement has come a long way in recapturing a new vision of the church defined by its classical marks: unity, holiness, catholicity, and apostolicity. The theme of unity for the sake of mission has taken root in all churches, although at times there are all too many signs of a sentimental ecumenism for its own sake. Similarly, the element of catholicity has recovered lost ground, and is quite pronounced in a new Lutheran self-understanding that defines itself as a reforming movement, not a Protestant denomination or sect, for the sake of the church catholic. And the mark of holiness is being rightly interpreted as being called and set apart in sacrificial service to others, rather than as withdrawal from the world in self-indulging religiousness and moral spotlessness.

With these classical marks of the church Luther placed cross, suffering, and martyrdom. *Crux probat omnia.* The horizontal and vertical bars of the cross symbolize the inseparable connectedness of evangelism announcing God's justification of sinners and social action advocating his justice for the poor. The cross has all too often been cloistered within the Sunday piety of the church, rather than being the dynamic of the everyday soldiers of the cross fighting for justice within the economic, social, and political situations of life.

Although there are other humanitarian groups at work to alleviate suffering and degradation, poverty and hunger, the church will want to be second to none in doing everything within its power to lift the burdens of the millions who starve, the races that are humiliated, the nations that are held captive, the classes that are deprived of full equality, etc. These aspects of the church's mission are commonly identified as humanization and development, meeting the needs of the poor and the oppressed and emphasizing liberation and advocacy. There is nothing unique about this type of church activity, except the spirit and motive by which it is done. Nevertheless, these concerns belong within the inclusive horizon of the church's mission.

But there is an aspect of the church's mission which is unique to the church. This is evangelism. If the church does not evangelize people who have not heard the good news, there is no one else in the world to do it. The evangelical thrust in the church's mission must be given a certain primacy and priority, not because souls are more important than bodies, or the next life than this life, for all come indivisibly from God and belong ultimately to him, but because God has given to the church a mandate which he has given to no other people in the world. This mandate is to preach the gospel of Christ. We can be positive about one sobering thought: If the church does not preach the message of salvation in the name of Christ to those who do not believe, no one else will. Christians are free to be politicians, business leaders, welfare workers, etc., but without them, there are still a lot of others to perform these necessary tasks. Christians alone have been called and ordained through their Baptism (the universal priesthood) to pass on the good news that all may hear. Faith comes from hearing (*fides ex auditu*). "But how are men to call upon him in whom they have not believed? And how are they to believe in him of whom they have never heard? And how are they to hear without a preacher? And how can men preach unless they are sent? As it is written, 'How beautiful are the feet of those who preach good news!' " (Rom. 10:14-15).

Stressing the uniqueness of evangelism among other missionary activities such as education, medical assistance, social service, and cultural enrichment must not become the occasion to fall back into the old dichotomies between sacred and secular, spiritual and physical, personal and political. Then the church's witness would fail to relate the kingdom of God to the totality of life in all its dimensions. What we are saying is that there is one essential dimension which is the unifying center of all others, without which there can be no holistic mission, and that is the message of God reconciling the world unto himself. The world does not know it, but it needs to hear this message. It is the most important thing the church can do for the world. It brings not only a positive therapeutic thrust into the lives of people, but also a powerful diagnostic voice into all areas of life, keeping ideas from becoming ideologies and ideals from becoming idols. The awareness of the transcendental kingdom of God as it came to expression in Jesus' ministry keeps Christians alert to the seductions of such idolatries as nationalism, communism, socialism, capitalism, militarism, and fascism. The church is in the world, but not of the world; its ultimate loyalty to Christ and his kingdom keeps every other involvement in the world relatively fluid and provisional.

Because Christ is Lord, the militant church marches under a higher loyalty than other groups and agencies. The church need not underestimate the magnitude of the struggles going on in the world. For its wrestling is not "against flesh and blood, but against the principalities, against the powers, against the world rulers of this present darkness, against the spiritual hosts of wickedness in the heavenly places" (Eph. 6:12). What does this mean? The church is prepared to take seriously the depth of sin and the power of the demonic in social and political life. This frees us from every sort of utopianism. The demonic forces are not easy to roust from one's personal life, church life, or life in the world.

As members of the one body of Christ, the church is a pilgrim people on the way to the nations, encountering diverse people of other loyalties. Not so long ago they were all summarily labeled idol-worshipers, seduced by Satan, heathen bound for hell, destined for the lake of fire that burns with brimstone (Rev. 19:20). These colorful but negative images do not provide the deep motive of mission in the encounter with the world religions. The motive is rather the positive conviction, born of the gospel, that Jesus Christ is the center and goal of world history. For this reason Christians will always go with the gospel to meet countless multitudes in other religions and ideologies and declare the name which is above all names, the Lord of the church and the Savior of the world.

Along with the abiding evangelistic task, Christians today are meeting the challenge of entering into dialog with people of other religions. This dialog is not a substitute for evangelism that blurs the distinction between Christian faith and other religious loyalties, resulting in syncretism. That would betray the uniqueness and finality of Jesus Christ. A Christ-centered evangelism that is of the essence of the church drives us onward to meet with people of other religions in coversation and dialog. Dialog is a good biblical word and was always a mode of apologetics in classical Christianity. In the book of Acts, Luke uses the word "dialog" (*dialegomai*) nine times to describe how Paul not only preached, but also reasoned, argued, persuaded, and discussed with people who did not share his faith in the gospel. As with Paul so with us, whether in evangelism or in dialog with non-Christians, Christ remains the center, and our commitment to the gospel is alive in our approach to people of other faiths. Our Christian approach must be human and humble, not paternalistic and triumphalistic, for in dialog we not only speak but listen for the sake of better understanding, lowering the profile of prejudice and opening the mind to new truth.

New challenges are continually arising to test the church's commitment to the mission of the gospel. When the church successfully meets a challenge, the door of history opens and the church goes forward in mission. Otherwise the door closes and the moment of opportunity is missed. The time of opportunity for mission has never been greater than it is now, in a world so full of international strife, racial hostility, religious wars, nuclear panic, moral decay, class conflict, and economic deprivation. It is in this kind of world that the church is called to be the light to the nations and the salt of the earth, to proclaim the gospel in Word and sacraments, and to serve people in every kind of need.

5

The Christian Future
in a Neopagan Society

The Pagan Ancestry of the West

A theological assessment of the church in the American context must take into account the role of religion in an advanced secularized society. We do not have in mind the idea of "secularity" in Friedrich Gogarten's sense as an authentic Christian development, but rather of "secularism" as an ideological phenomenon that attempts to comprehend all of reality, including religion, within its own immanental framework. So thorough is this process of secularization within American culture that some voices are sounding the need to reevangelize our pagan society.[1]

The prophetic words of W. A. Visser't Hooft in an article, "Evangelism in the Neo-Pagan Situation," clearly apply to America as well as Europe. "It is high time that Christians recognize that they are confronted with a new paganism. . . . Christians have been very slow to recognize the pagan elements in modern culture. They were so convinced that the Western world was a Christianized world that they could not make themselves believe that pagan forces could possibly exert a big influence in its midst. So they tried to console themselves by arguing that the new pagans were really Christians who expressed themselves in a somewhat different manner.''[2] Then he goes on to say that the so-called Christian nations of the West must now become new mission fields, and that the churches have not really begun to face the challenge of neopaganism.[3]

The new paganism is in many ways to be seen as the reemergence of the pagan sources of Western civilization. The spiritual ancestry of the West reaches back to sources that antedate Christianity, namely, to pagan sources originating in Greece and Iran. The vision of the meaning and destiny of society operative in Western civilization is not modeled exclusively on the Christian vision that sought to displace or fulfill the earlier pagan options. Christianity in the West became a confluence of several streams of religious symbols, some of them coming from pagan sources. Syncretism has become a word that many would like to avoid, but one can hardly deny that the history of Western Christianity has been, after all, the story of both the success and the failure of syncretism. In a series of steps Christianity became Hellenistic, Roman, Germanic, Nordic, Anglo-Saxon, and finally American. At times the identification of Christianity with its local culture has been excessive, offering glaring examples of false indigenousness so that ''the salt has lost its savor.'' Is this not now the problem of Western Christianity? In the United States many have complained that Christianity has degenerated in some places into a kind of ''civil religion,'' providing ideological legitimation to national patriotic crusades, particularly in times of war. The alliance of the Reagan administration with the ''moral majority'' and ''born again'' religion is the latest example of how this can work.

Did Christianity ever fully digest and transform Greek philosophy under the impact of the gospel, or did Christianity provide a general glaze which covered up the continuing virility of pagan culture below the surface of the imperial Christian establishment? The Greek ideal was, above all, humanistic. Again and again the humanistic image erupts in the midst of Christianity, as in the Renaissance, the Enlightenment, 19th-century socialism, and 20th-century neo-Marxist revolutionary ideology. How could these movements emerge on the soil of Christian Europe, except for the fact they were linked to a vision of human dignity and a system of values embedded in Greek culture? In this system "man" is at the center; "man" is the measure of all things. During the flowering of Greek culture, a shift takes place from the realm of the gods to the world of human beings. Greek art, religion, political thought, and science were based on the values of ideal humanity, on the ideal human community, on the concepts of beauty, liberty, virtue, truth, and justice. Greek culture provided a prototype of all succeeding humanistic images of human being and human community that periodically erupted in the Christian West.

The spiritual riches of Greece spread in ever-widening circles through the whole Mediterranean world. The utopia of the ideal state lived on in the Hellenistic world empire of Alexander the Great, representing a vision of an ideal reign of peace. This vision of an ideal earthly state lived on in the Roman Empire, which in its turn influenced European thought for centuries to come. In addition to Greece, then, the Roman Empire left its stamp on the budding young faith. The vision of a universal empire, primarily geographical in nature, and its corollary of the *pax romana* mingled with biblical Christian eschatological symbols, leading ultimately to imperialistic and triumphalistic images of the place of Christendom in world history, right up to the recent colonialistic adventures of most Western nations.

Christianity and the Rise of Apostasy

When we look at primitive Christianity in its original setting, we are viewing only one link in a chain of images concerning the meaning and destiny of life that have given substance and form to Western civilization. The other links in the chain have never been broken but only tinted by a process of gold-plated evangelization, frequently inspired by military and political force. But just as demons cannot be exorcised by the gun, neither could competing spiritual images of human meaning and destiny be overcome by the establishment of Christianity as the imperially favored religion.

Christianity began as a two-dimensional reality, of Jesus and the kingdom and of Christ and the gospel. It cannot be reduced to one of these two poles without massive reductionism, yielding either an

Ebionite picture based on the Synoptics or a docetic picture based on the Epistles. The identity and meaning of Christianity lie in the unity of these two dimensions. If Jesus taught the triptych of repentance-conversion-forgiveness, Paul taught that of cross-resurrection-redemption, and both sets of three became wonderfully welded together in apostolic preaching and later in patristic theology. The Christian vision of the meaning and destiny of humanity and society makes the best of both worlds. The awe-inspiring dynamism of Christianity in its youth commingled images both individual and collective, earthly and heavenly, material and spiritual, cosmic and cultic, apocalyptic and metaphysical. Christianity seems to have lost its spiritual power whenever it opted for one side or the other.

The historical reality of Christianity has managed to survive throughout centuries of ups and downs, sometimes threatened by fundamental alterations of its basic structure, other times recapturing the power of the original gospel. The so-called Middle Ages have been viewed by both Protestants and humanists as a stationary period of dark times. They have been called the "Dark Ages," and any antiquated idea is dubbed "medieval." On the contrary, these centuries were a dynamic period, and there was considerable tension between contrasting views of the meaning and destiny of life and of the role of the church in the world. Western Christianity was shaped in the medium of the Middle Ages. Images from the past Hellenistic-Iranian-Jewish-Christian heritage were carried over into Western culture and influenced the future course of events. It is false to look on this period as a Catholic monolith. Sticks of dynamite were planted here and there with the potentiality to blow up the whole Roman and Catholic Empire. Seeds were sown which produced movements vastly different from each other, such as the Reformation, the Renaissance, the Revolution, and later Romanticism. Consider the revolutionary seeds sown by Joachim of Fiore, who was the spiritual father of a movement Kant later labeled "philosophical chiliasm," and which reached its climax in G. E. Lessing. It was the Joachimites who made the electrifying statement that the papal church is the church of the Antichrist.

After the Reformation, chiliasm blazed up into a roaring fire of revolution. Thomas Münzer was the forerunner of socialism, but he was inspired by the writing of Joachim in *The Eternal Gospel* (*Evangelium Aeternum*). Biblical eschatology was translated into a socialist utopia that can be realized here and now. From the viewpoint of chiliastic enthusiasm, the Reformation was a bitter disappointment; its hopes for historical and social transformation were a lukewarm affair. The chiliasts were declared heretical by both the Reformation and the Counter-Reformation. However, their ideals were not extinguished, but prepared the way for modern times, particularly in its antichurchly forms of utopian socialism, Marxist communism, and anarchism. In this line of development, chiliasm becomes thoroughly secularized and enormously influential on the future of Western culture.

Just as there was a Christian form of chiliasm that became secularized and anti-Christian, so also there was a Christian form of humanism in the Renaissance that eventually liberated itself from any heteronomous alliance with the authority of the church and its supernatural revelation. The *Theologia Platonica* of the Florentine Academy tried to infuse Christianity with Platonism along humanistic lines. The utopias of Thomas Moore (*Utopia*), Francis Bacon (*New Atlantis*), and Campanella (*City of the Sun*) were signs that the established social order and the existing political institutions were no longer considered sacrosanct and unalterable but rather provisional human creations, subject to the demands of history and open to new things. According to humanism, the present is the time for new things, and human beings can make things new by their own efforts. The church was no longer seen as an impregnable fortress to be feared, and when the church allied itself in modern revolutionary times against the forces that called for change, it came to be seen more and more as an anachronism.

The humanistic thrust of the Renaissance was carried further during the age of Enlightenment, and took many and various antichurchly turns. In England we see outbreakings of empiricism, positivism, and deism; in France materialism, pantheism, and atheism; in Germany rationalism, naturalism, and romanticism. These labels cover a lot of history we cannot pursue here, but together they reveal the magnitude of apostasy that was mounting against the church and the Christian faith. These are movements that virulently sought to detach Europe from its Christian connection. In the Enlightenment the focus is on human society, human happiness, and general human welfare. Religion appears as deism or as natural religion—reasonable, tolerant, unchurchly, and unbiblical. Whatever is good and worthy in traditional Christianity is blended into this "religion within the limits of reason alone" (Kant). The pagan roots of Western civilization were beginning to pose a serious challenge to the biblical sources of Christianity.

The spirit of the Enlightenment was a rebellion against orthodox Christianity, but it was not yet revolutionary. The revolutionary mind matured in the 19th century, and took an openly hostile anti-Christian attitude. Radical and revolutionary socialism capitalized on the alienation of the masses against the organized church, tied in as it was with the structures of power, privilege, stability, and order. Marxism came along with promises of no more cries of unemployment, hunger, poverty, and domination by the ruling class. Capital itself will be held in common as a property of the people, and finally the state, with its false authority and coercive power, will wither away. A new humanity and a new community will be born to last forever. The kingdom of God without God will be realized at last on earth.

Paul Tillich and others desperately tried to reconcile Christianity and socialism in the movement called "religious socialism." But the movement failed, as Tillich himself confessed. The forces of National Socialism, rather than religious socialism, took charge of the times and filled the void. The new spirit of nationalism was just one more bit of evidence that Christianity had lost its grip on the soul of the masses. The churches were impotent in the face of Hitler, and the pope fared no better in the face of Mussolini. Paganism in new forms began to run riot in the first half of the 20th century.

In the realm of ideas, theology, once the queen of the sciences, steadily lost ground to philosophy, its appointed handmaiden. Just a brief list of the names tells the story, from Rousseau to Comte, from La Mettrie to Voltaire, from Darwin to Marx, from Goethe to Lessing, from Kant to Fichte, from Feuerbach to Nietzsche. In various and sundry ways these names represent a litany of anti-Christian trends that nourish the repaganization of the West. One conclusion seems to have been drawn: If the God of orthodox Christianity takes the side of the existing order, it is an idol to be overthrown with the rest of the social order, and will give way to something really new. But Christians at the time did not take seriously the full measure of the apostasy that was growing to gigantic proportions in their very midst. In the encyclopedia, *Religion in Geschichte und Gegenwart* (first edition, 1913), the article on Goethe closes by calling him "the first representative of the Christianity of the future," and yet Goethe made it clear that he was "a convinced non-Christian." It remained for Nietzsche to cry out, "God is dead," meaning that the God of the Christians is dead and the churches have become tombs. And what were the churches doing meanwhile? They were involved in endless religious controversies, and the case for Christianity seemed to be in full retreat before all the onrushing rejuvenated forces of classical paganism.

The Modern Search for Christian Identity

According to Arnold Toynbee's interpretation of history, the culture that survives is the one that can make a timely and adequate response to the ever-new challenges that are presented to it. We have described the neopagan challenges to the dominant place of Christianity in the scheme of things in the West. It seems clear that the Christian response does not yet appear to have been either timely or adequate enough. But the score of the future has not yet been decided, and we are still in the middle of the ball game. We shall have to ask the question, finally, whether a revival of the Christian mission in Western civilization is still possible, and under what conditions.

The history of Christianity could be written as not so much the Christianization of the West as the Western amalgamation of Christianity. Søren Kierkegaard looked out upon Christian Europe and had the gall to ask whether New Testament Christianity still existed anywhere. It was a rhetorical question. He believed that Christianity had contracted a terminal illness. It is interesting that 150 years later, we are perhaps only now ready to take his question seriously. His *Attack on Christendom* was motivated by a desire to see a new birth of authentic faith. Christianity began as an eschatological faith,[4] anchored historically in Jesus' proclamation of the rapidly approaching kingdom of God and the apostolic preaching of Jesus as the messianic bringer of the kingdom, based on his cross and resurrection. The early church had to adjust to the disappointment of having to reckon with a postponement of the speedy return of Christ to this world.

The problem that faces modern Christianity is different from that. The modern problem is that the Christian belief in the future has suffered an eroding rationalization process, so that the eschatological idea itself has been eliminated from a modern view of how God relates to the world of human life and society. Not only is any expectation of the final advent of Christ discounted, but no expectation of a future transformation of God's created world seems to have survived, except strangely with a handful of otherworldly sects. It would be necessary to give an extensive account of the history of theology up to the present to document this contention. The eschatological dimension of Christianity, fundamental to its very identity and meaning, has been eroded or demolished under the impact of the trends we have traced out in the previous section—naturalism, rationalism, materialism, empiricism, etc.

Jacob Taubes concludes his study of *Abendländische Eschatologie*—in my view one of the most interesting books on Western cultural history—with a discussion of Hegel, Kierkegaard, and Marx, in which he maintains that with them eschatology has petered out. He thus confirms Troeltsch's famous statement: "The eschatological bureau is closed these days." When Albert Schweitzer rediscovered eschatology, it was only with respect to primitive Christianity and not at all with respect to its significance for Christianity today. As someone has said, "Schweitzer was not a member of his own school of thought." A Jewish sociologist, not a Christian theologian, has written: "It can be said without exaggeration that every eschatological study which has appeared since the time of Schweitzer has systematically, if unconsciously, negated and destroyed eschatology while ostensibly supporting it."[5] It took the non-Christian existentialist, Karl Jaspers, to call the bluff of the Christian theologian, Rudolf Bultmann, for taking the eschaton out of eschatology.[6] Theologians from many schools of thought have been attempting in like manner to deeschatologize Christianity. Theologians have valiantly tried to retain the Bible as God's revelation, minus its stumbling block of an eschatological future causally related to the course of historical events. The chapter in dogmatics dealing with *ta eschata* (the end events) has been getting shorter and shorter. Even Karl Barth had nothing left in reserve for volume 5 of his *Church Dogmatics*. When he came to eschatology, which had been planned for volume 5, he found that he had already said it all.

To experience Jesus Christ and his gospel anew in our time, the heart of authentic Christian faith, we must attend to the twin pillars of this faith, namely, belief in God and belief in the coming kingdom of God. Belief in Christ without God is as useless for Christian faith as belief in God without Christ; and belief in the gospel without the kingdom is as illusory as belief in the kingdom without the gospel. But just here is where the theological efforts at *resourcement* seem to be having the greatest difficulty. As we have already indicated, Schweitzer, at the beginning of this century, inaugurated a deeschatologizing process which ended in an ethical revision of the gospel. He eliminated the kingdom as an act of divine intervention and replaced it by a humanistic goal of human self-fulfillment by the moral will and the striving of humanity (ethical voluntarism). His argument: The modern mind lacks the capacity to share the eschatological worldview of Jesus and primitive Christianity. He ends by believing in Jesus the man, whose teachings still contain somehow the highest values worthy of human striving.

Since Schweitzer there has been one attempt after the other to recover the essence of eschatology that makes sense in modern terms. Karl Barth tried, and he stated: "Christianity that is not entirely and altogether eschatology has entirely and altogether nothing to do with Christ."[7] Barth succeeded in raising once again the question of how to tap the current that comes from the eschatological dynamo of biblical Christian faith. Rudolf Bultmann tried but, under the label of demythologizing, the eschatological images were replaced by existentialist ideas. In the United States process theology has become popular, but this follows the same road of deeschatologizing. The countereschatological trends of modern theology that began with Schleiermacher have reached their zenith in the various ethical, existential, axiological, praxiological, and transcendental interpretations of the Christian gospel. They are all prescriptions that leave the patient with a sickness unto death. It is not possible for us further to chart the course of development of eschatology to the present time within the limits of this chapter. Enough has been said to indicate where the problem lies and the point at which a breakthrough will have to occur. Are there any theological impulses around that will resist the creeping secularization of the kingdom of God as an eschatological realm of God's powerful future impacting on the world in judgment and grace? Is there still a future for the eschatological future of which the Bible speaks within the dying civilization of Christendom?[8]

Karl Heim once wrote: "Belief in God and belief in the End are inseparable" ("*Gottesglauben und Endglauben sind unzertrennlich*").[9] In my opinion this is a strikingly pertinent observation. A God without his future becomes a future without God. Countereschatological theology leads to death-of-God theology. The end of belief in the End leads to the beginning of the end of belief in God— as the Omega Point! An eschatology without *eschaton* is the twin of a theology without *theos*. If God is not alive as the future end of time and history, then God is dead, and history can run on endlessly as if God did not exist. From a Christian point of view, the future of God and the future of salvation for this world hang by the same thread.

Is it not relevant that the iconoclastic deeschatologizing of Christianity happened hand in hand, at the same time and in the same place, as the announcement of the death of God? Of course, Christians cannot believe in a future without the living God. At most we are open to a discussion of the future of Christianity in the West, the future of the so-called Christian nations, or the future of the organized churches. For many people in the West, Christianity already has its future behind it; it no longer represents a live option. Its system of rituals and beliefs has already become a matter of concern to a dwindling minority. Here is one statistic to give us pause. Only 15% of West German Protestants regularly attend Sunday worship,[10] and it is even worse in some other European countries.

If the gospel has lost its eschatological vitamins, what is left to nourish the people? Perhaps the gospel may still be a consolation for a few individuals, even when the power of its promise to transform humanity and the world has been cancelled by a rationalizing synthesis or a demythologizing hermeneutic.

Toward a Christian Counteroffensive

What does it mean to say that "God is dead"? It may mean that our picture of the world has no place for God. God is among the unemployed; he has retired; he has been pensioned off. It means that our thinking about history, philosophy, and science has made a radical shift from a theocentric to an anthropocentric worldview. It means that God is removed from the stream of temporal events. The destruction of the historical dynamics of the eschatological gospel makes Christianity appear like an antique, yellow with age. Some people like antiques; a few are in the business of selling antiques, while others are collectors with aesthetic interests.

What should be the church's response to the challenge of our secularized culture? What are the chances of a revival in Western society of Christian faith? The demographic projections are not brimming with optimism. It seems that by the method of trend extrapolation things will have to get worse before they could possibly get better. There seems to be an unstoppable trend towards the gradual and eventual disappearance of the Christian faith as the traditional religion of the West. It is only an impression, but we sense that we are approaching the hour of darkness at noon. We could be wrong and we hope we are. Where people used to believe that God would ultimately bring about the end of the world, now an unbelieving world claims that it has brought about the end of God. What is the future of Christian faith in such a context?

The future is not very promising unless the church finds a way to put into active operation a counteroffensive, to bring new life into the decaying body of Western religious culture. Some propose that all we have to do is to modernize the old concepts, to find new language and new modes of thinking, to adapt them to our times.

Others believe that we ought not yield an inch, but counteract modernism with every available resource. The one side proposes a modernizing apologetic for Christian faith, and the other side a conservative orthodox restoration. But I do not believe that we can turn back the clock. We cannot restore the past; we must move forward with the times, although we may oppose them in light of an alternative future that we anticipate. There is no reason for us to exclude in advance the possibility of a comeback of the Christian option in the West. One cannot exclude the possibility of a miracle even in these pragmatic and realistic times, these scientific and technological times.

What are the conditions of the possibility of such a miracle? First I believe that we must count heavily on the success of the ecumenical movement. This movement is propelled by faith in the reality of the *una sancta* that calls for visible embodiment. The recovery of the unity of the church is a precondition for reconstituting the Christian mission in Europe and America or anywhere else in the world today. After unity is achieved, we must ask, for what? Unity is a means to an end, not the end in itself. According to the gospel message, in the words of our Lord, it is "that the world might believe."

Are there some other counterforces that are working for the renewal of the Christian faith and the church's mission? In addition to ecumenical efforts the churches must continue their theological efforts "to get the message straight," and take care that they do not pervert the gospel or preach a different gospel than what they have received from the apostles (Gal. 1:6-12). But what if they are "turning to a different gospel"? Paul says, "Let them be accursed."

Many Christians in Europe are calling for the disestablishment of the church, to liberate it finally from the role it was assigned as a state religion in the age of Christendom. The state is blessed in many ways by the church, and the church is privileged in many ways by the state. It is a sweet deal, and it will be difficult to bring about the kind of separation that would most certainly augur better for both. From an American perspective, we tend to see a separation of church and state as inevitable in a pluralistic secular society, and we believe that a church organized on the principle of voluntarism is in the long run healthier.

Of course, the church is not called to live in isolation from the world. If the church is being called upon to separate itself from "unholy alliances," it must be for the sake of making a new advance in mission to the world. The church ought to be a sacrament of hope for the world's future. The church is needed as the voice of prophecy in the world to regenerate the social and political images that inspire the world to pursue the ways of civil righteousness, peace, harmony, and justice. The church cannot limit its mission to an evangelism that seeks to salvage individuals from either burning hell or a meaningless world. The church works not only *in* history but *for* history, not only *in* culture but *for* culture, and not only diagnostically in words of law and judgment, but therapeutically in gospel words of hope and healing.

What counts in a theology of mission and evangelism is not merely another theory about the world, but another way of action for the world. The church as the community of believers needs to be renewed, needs a new formation, not only a re-formation. This calls for a new sense of mission, expressing itself as liberation, lifting burdens, opening roads, expanding horizons, helping people out of slavery, and showing them the way home.

Perhaps the crisis of Christianity in the West is much more serious than we have glimpsed. We must prepare ourselves for a future in which the megatrends leading to disintegration seem to be gathering momentum, while the counterforces directed at regeneration in the life of the church seem feeble by comparison. All Christians around the world have much at stake in the present plight of Christianity in Western society.

6

Praxis: The New Key to Christian Mission?

On Making Models of Theology

Praxis has become a key word in modern theology. Gustavo Gutierrez writes in *A Theology of Liberation* that theology is a critical reflection on praxis that drives toward liberation of the world.[1] Praxis has also become a key word in mapping various theological options today. David Tracy in *Blessed Rage for Order* has tried to bring order into our understanding of pluralism by drawing a map of five types of theology.[2] He prefers to call them models. The five basic models are the orthodox, the liberal, the neoorthodox, the radical, and the revisionist. Each of these types generates its own theory of praxis. In Tracy's typology it turns out that the neoorthodox model encompasses both the theologians of hope and the theologians of liberation. Thus Moltmann and Gutierrez, as well as Metz and Segundo, stem from the same neoorthodox model, but the Latin Americans radicalize more its political implications. Tracy refers to all these and others, including Alves, Shaull, Soelle, and me, as eschatological theologians of praxis.

The chief result of Tracy's typology is the construction of a new revisionist option for theology, which he claims is not only more radical than eschatological theology in its theory of praxis but far more rigorously critical in its appropriation of the classical Christian symbols. The essential outcome of critical revisionism over against the eschatological theology of praxis is at least threefold, according to Tracy.[3] First, eschatological theology of praxis is shown to be derived from neoorthodoxy because it clings essentially to the God of classical theism; second, it betrays the Christocentricity of the neoorthodox greats like Barth, Bultmann, and Tillich; and third, it has not given up the traditional claim of a special revelation. Tracy's revisionist model is distinctly different in having abandoned these marks of neoorthodoxy, which he finds repristinated in some fashion in both the theologians of hope and the theologians of liberation. Tracy then proceeds to argue that his own revisionist model employs critical-theoretical rigor,[4] both in analyzing the meaning of the main Christian symbols, like God, Christ, and revelation, and in providing a critical theory of society, matching that of the Frankfurt School. It is clear from Tracy's discussion that the revisionist theologian wants to lay claim to praxis as a new magic word for our time, although nowhere is the content of such praxis spelled out.

Another theologian, Matthew Lamb, has drawn a different map of theological models or types, using the idea of the relation of theory and praxis as the key tool of analysis.[5] He agrees with Tracy that there are five types, but he disagrees on what they are. The first is the orthodox model, the same as Tracy's first type. It holds to the primacy of theory; it deduces praxis from theory. The second type affirms, in contrast, the primacy of praxis; it reduces theory to praxis. Lamb combines in this type the liberal and radical models in Tracy's scheme. Lamb's third model corresponds to Barth's type of neoorthodoxy, which places Christian faith totally outside all theory and praxis in a relation of sheer shock; there is simply no point of identity with human theory and praxis. Lamb's fourth and fifth types are more interesting. His fifth type does to Tracy what Tracy did to the theologians of hope and liberation in lumping them all together with neoorthodoxy. Lamb calls his fourth type "Critical Theoretic Correlations," collapsing Tracy's revisionist claim into a large class of thinkers who have tried to correlate the essence of Christianity with the modern world. What makes Tracy's revisionism into a distinctively fifth type disappears, making it simply one more variant of the theoretical correlation approach that produced such different results in Bultmann, Tillich, the Niebuhrs, Rahner, and more lately Pannenberg.

Lamb's fifth type is called "Critical Praxis Correlations." It is obviously the one he favors. Here in the fifth type, praxis becomes the basis of theory. This fifth type differs from the second "Primacy of Praxis" type in that it does not restrict praxis to a particular kind of historical action, conceived in narrow Marxist terms. Nevertheless, it does postulate some kind of orthopraxis as the foundation of orthodoxy; it does look for correlations with Christianity at the point of emancipating praxis rather than of philosophical theory. The political theology in Europe (Moltmann, Metz, and Soelle) and the liberation theology of South America (Gutierrez, Segundo, Dussel, Bonino, and Assmann) are the best-known representatives of this fifth type.

The interesting thing in both these typologies is that they shove sharply opposed positions into the same cubbyhole. In Tracy's typology, Barth, Bultmann, and Tillich all stand together in light of his revisionist perspective. Equally odd in Tracy's typology is that among the "good guys" in the revisionist camp are such strange bedfellows as Andrew Greeley and Schubert Ogden, Michael Novak and Gordon Kaufman, Leslie Dewart and Van Harvey, Gregory Baum and Langdon Gilkey. It is difficult for me to see the tie that binds all these thinkers together, except that each is revising in his own way the tradition in which he stands. But who then is not a revisionist in that sense? Not to be a revisionist would mean being a pure repristinationist, which characterizes almost nobody. Lamb's typology is more useful because he gives us the key principle by which his distinctions are drawn, namely, the theory/praxis relationship. Even so he has to do a lot of shoving to cram all modern theologies into his five boxes.

I do not wish to focus on the tour de force involved in either Lamb's or Tracy's typologies. I would rather call into question whether the crack that has opened up between the European political theologians and the South American liberation theologians is so slight that they can be embraced by the same type. It is well known that the liberation theologians have been critical of the European theologians of hope, and vice versa. The typologies of Lamb and Tracy both tend to cover up the rifts that have occurred in 20th-century theology. In the case of Tracy, it is the rift between Barth and Bultmann or between Tillich and both of them. In the case of Lamb it is now the growing rift between the European-based eschatological theologies and the South American-based liberation theologies. That rift has to do essentially with the use of Marx, his critical theory of society, and the way in which theology is related to praxis. This rift is decisive for the way in which praxis is understood in terms of the Christian mission in the world. What determines the meaning of Christian praxis, the gospel or ideology?

The Trojan Horse of Liberation Theology

What Marxism has not been able to accomplish in a frontal attack on Christianity as a religion now threatens to come to pass by means of a word that can smuggle the Marxist critique of religion inside the walls of Christian theology. For this reason I am dubbing praxis the Trojan horse of liberation theology. It has often happened in history that the threat to Christian identity does not arise from those who explicitly attack it from the outside, but from those who launch an invasion of Christianity in a Trojan horse. Only when the horse is inside the walls of Troy does the hatch open and Agamemnon and all the rest jump out and capture the city. The Marxist critique of religion from the outside has not been able to succeed; but if its critical theory of praxis can spread inside the body of Christianity, it might be able to claim victory at last.

Christianity is vulnerable. It has left itself wide open to the accusation that its theology is both too theoretical and too ideological, without generating an emancipatory praxis in the social sphere. No wonder that on its left flank the idea of praxis would be welcomed as a way of linking Christianity to a movement that promises to change the world for the better. The word *praxis* itself is not one that we find in the vocabulary of the Christian tradition. It was first introduced into philosophy by a Polish philosopher, August von Cieszkowski, who was one of the Young Hegelians, along with Karl

Marx. In 1838 Cieszkowski said that the future role of philosophy was "to become a practical philosophy or rather a philosophy of practical activity, of praxis, exercising a direct influence on social life and developing the future in the realm of concrete activity."[6] Here praxis acquires its special meaning by being played off against mere theory operating in the rarefied atmosphere of speculation. Marx laid hold of the idea of praxis in his criticism of Hegel. Hegel was satisfied with right understanding, but the task before us can be discharged only by means of practical activity.[7] Hegel's philosophy is something that has been realized only in the German cranium, in a kind of dream history; it has not been realized in the real life of the nation.[8] True emancipation can be realized only in practice.

Marx's notion of praxis has been mediated to current liberation theology through the works of neo-Marxists, the best known of whom are members of the Frankfurt school, people such as Adorno, Horkheimer, and Habermas. The influence of Marcuse and Bloch must also be mentioned. Any differences between Marx and these neo-Marxists are pretty much overshadowed by their common notion of praxis as the aim of philosophy and the kind of action bent on changing the world. The point of philosophy is not to contemplate the world but to pull the trigger that will bring about freedom and rationality, overturning the existing order.

Gustavo Gutierrez defines theology as a critical theory of praxis.[9] The phase is catching on. But what does it mean and does it bode well for Christian theology? Praxis has become the key to understanding Marxism; it has also made a great impact on European political theology and the theology of liberation. Moltmann, who has had the greatest theological influence on the liberation theologians, has said, "The new criterion of theology and of faith is to be found in praxis."[10] J. B. Metz similarly has written, "A new relation between theory and practice, between knowledge and morality, between reflection and revolution, will have to be worked out, and it will have to determine theological thought, if theological thought is not to be left at a precritical stage. Henceforth, practical and, in the widest sense of the word, political reason must take part in all critical reflection in theology."[11] There are numerous such statements in all the books of the liberation theologians. I also have encouraged taking up the idea of praxis as a corrective of traditional theology whose ethic, because it never challenged the coercive and violent structural dimensions of society, actually contributed to the preservation of the status quo. I have recommended the adoption of the notion of praxis as a kind of supplement to the basic hermeneutical operations of theology which necessarily come first. A theology that takes up the idea of the kingdom of God as Jesus proclaimed it might do well to link its eschatology to the notion of praxis. I have therefore coined the word *eschatopraxis*,[12] joining eschatology and praxis, to express the biblical notion that eschatological truth is not idle fantasy but something to be done here and now. The First Epistle of John speaks of "doing the truth."[13] It is impossible to be overly practical in expressing the life that has been transformed by the power of God's love and truth and that throbs with the impulses of faith and hope. It is time for theology to make a positive turn to praxis, despite the fact of its Marxist provenance.

A Critique of the Critical Theory of Praxis

I am suggesting that liberation theology is not sufficiently critical in its adoption of the critical theory of praxis that stems from Marxism. It speaks a lot about being critical, but it is not sufficiently critical, except of theologies made in Europe and America. It is not self-critical. Liberation theology has been relentless in its attack on traditional theology for its political ineffectiveness. All of the theories and interpretations of traditional theology have left the world just as it is. The slogans of Marx and Marxism are so attractive because they clearly demand a union of critical theory and liberating praxis. Access to the truth can be had only through an activity directed to transforming society. All other ideas—religious, ethical, or philosophical—are so much ideology apart from concrete emancipatory praxis.

Liberation theology has called for a shift from metaphysics to politics, precisely in order to ground its theology in praxis. Habermas of the Frankfurt school has pointed out that every critical theory becomes a "new ideology" once it becomes dissociated from praxis and thus loses its critical power.[14] The irony is that many people have jumped on the bandwagon of liberation theology, learning a new rhetoric about critical theory and critical praxis. Then liberation theology becomes an impotent protest when it becomes the latest fashion consumed by alienated theologians and their students in capitalist countries. Liberation theology is thus in danger of becoming a mere ideology of the left just as the traditional dogmatic theology became, in the eyes of liberation theologians, the unselfconscious reflection of the ideology of the right.

Christian theology has good reason to be on guard against the danger of dragging the Trojan horse inside the walls. Marx became so enthusiastic about the possibilities of revolutionary praxis that he was ready to see it as the fulfillment of philosophy, and therefore its very abolition. Marx's term is the same as Hegel's, *Aufhebung*.[15] The term has been translated as "negation" or as "abolition." Both are misleading, for the *Aufhebung* of philosophy implies its inner fulfillment, and therefore yields a positive result. In Hegel the *Aufhebung*, literally translated as the "sublation" of philosophy, is absolute knowledge; in Marx it is critical praxis. This is the word of Marx: "Let us state it openly: in being realized, philosophy is abolished (*aufgehoben*); it reaches its end, that is, its goal and final achievement. It ceases to be."[16] I call this notion a sign of enthusiasm, in Luther's sense of *Schwärmerei*. Luther applied this term to the Müntzerites, whom Marxists see as their only 16th-century precursors. The Müntzerites believed that they were ushering in at last the age of the Spirit and were glowing with spiritual enthusiasm. So Luther spoke sarcastically of the *Schwärmer* who had swallowed the Holy Spirit, feathers and all.

This Marxist notion of the sublation of philosophy into praxis has also worked like acid to dissolve much of the substance of classical theology into a very narrow focus on the historical praxis of human beings in history, leading to the transformation of the world in social and economic terms. This orientation has led to the claim that faith will be "veri-fied" by doing the right thing, that is by orthopraxis.[17] This praxial concern accounts for the virtually complete restoration of the ethical concept of the kingdom of God that prevailed in Ritschlian circles at the end of the 19th century, along with an anti-metaphysical bent which dismisses everything beyond history and ethics as hazy idealistic superstructure. We can thus recognize in liberation theology a parallel tendency toward an *Aufhebung* of theology into praxis as its basis, goal, and truth. Such a claim for praxis seems overly optimistic in a world in which every praxis, including the praxis of the best moralists or zealots old and new, can at most be an *approximation* of the absolute future of God's kingdom and can never be realized in a utopia here on earth. The liberation theologians have placed too great a trust in praxis, and thus we find glowing statements like this one from Gutierrez; "The social praxis of contemporary man has begun to reach maturity."[18] Where are these contemporary human beings who carry so much promise for emancipatory praxis? In Russia? In the United States? In China?

The neo-Marxist critical theory of praxis claims to have gotten rid of an a priori ideal image of human being which calls for implementation in real action. The traditional sequence has placed being before action, theory prior to praxis, faith ahead of works, etc. The critical theory of praxis reverses the order. Praxis is given precedence over any theory that is based on a positive image of human being taken from a theology or philosophy of history. Critical theory of praxis, therefore, claims to be purely scientific, analytically developed in the context of struggle and opposition to an oppressive and violent society. A prior positive definition of the nature and destiny of human being is dismissed by the critical theory of praxis. Neither the past nor the future hold for us a positive picture of humanity and society. We can only struggle in the present by contestation and contradiction; the essence of humanity and the good society can be reflected only by means of the "negative dialectic." Can such an idea of praxis be taken over into Christian theology without being baptized and thereby critically purged of its Marxist orientation?

The critical theory of praxis assumes that it is right to change the world. It was Max Stirner who put the question to Marx, "But why change the world?"[19] Does not an answer to this question mean that underlying the demand for change, some prior claim is being made about the nature of humanity and the world? Can a positive answer to this question be deduced by a rational empirical scientific analysis of the negative conditions of life in the concrete present? To call for change and to claim that such is both possible and necessary presupposes a fundamental commitment to freedom as a positive ideal with prior ontological validity. Mere analysis of existing structures cannot by itself yield a verdict that they are oppressive unless such analysis is guided by a prior hermeneutical commitment to freedom as the essence of being human.

Since the idea of freedom cannot be derived from the empirical state of affairs—for Marx was correct in asserting that people and their societies are not yet free—then whence this idea of freedom? For us this idea of freedom has been released into history through the promises of God and inscribed in the basic symbols of the Bible and the Christian tradition. We already have before us the story of our freedom in which we are invited to participate through faith. This is an existential experience bound up with the Christian claim that the freedom of God has already been released into history through the person and activity of Jesus the Christ. The Marxist orientation in the liberation theology of praxis tends to place the freedom for which we strive purely in the category of the ''not yet,'' thus leaping over the all-important ''already'' actualized in the past historical event on which Christianity is based.

Liberation theologians hold that theology is essentially a critical theory of praxis. We must insist, however, on the priority of the hermeneutical aspect of theology which reflects not on present praxis but on past history insofar as that history conveys the symbols charged with the promises of God and the hopes of freedom for humanity and the world. Praxis is really a second step inspired by the hermeneutical retrieval of a past laden with the story of God's interventions on humanity's behalf. It is unrealistic to claim that we could discover what is *orthos* in our praxis as the ground and criterion of what is true in theology. Such talk has a Pelagian ring to it. Should we jump from the frying pan of an orthodoxy into the fire of an orthopraxy which could be equally confining and heteronomous?

Postcritical orthopraxy is no more enchanting than precritical orthodoxy for people who have found that freedom for which Christ has set them free. The Christian gospel generates its own form of freedom; it does not wait upon a liberating praxis to make it true and meaningful. One aspect of the freedom generated by the gospel is the freedom to use the critical theory of praxis to one's heart's content, but without raising it to the dignity of a soteriological category. Christian theology at its best has always claimed the right to "despoil the Egyptians," to use any concept or tool or insight in the pagan world and integrate it into a circle of meaning in which Christ stands in the center and his cross is the criterion. Rather than saying that theology *is* a critical theory of praxis, it is more appropriate to state that Christian theology is free at this stage of history to develop critical correlations with the theory of praxis that stems from Marxism. But the Marxist theory of praxis will have to pass through the fires of purgatory to make it useful for Christian theology. Liberation theologians must do to Marx and Marxism what Thomas did to Aristotle and Aristotelianism—that is, transform the categories in light of the biblical message and Christian truth.

The Marxist idea of praxis is at least partly responsible for the way in which liberation theology flattens out certain dimensions of Christian theology. Think of the liturgical and mystical dimensions of Christian faith. The abysmal aspect in the experience of God as the *mysterium tremendum et fascinosum* is conspicuously absent in liberation theology. The mystery of God is the power to arouse awe, silence, prayer, and praise. No critical theory of praxis in the Marxist sense can give meaning to this purely doxological aspect of Christian language. Reducing theology to the pole of praxis is defective. While it accelerates the meaning of work and weekday activity, it robs faith of the meaning of rest and Sabbath worship. The motifs of mystery and divine transcendence are diminished in the radical reduction of the meaning of God to the dialectics of the historical process.

The themes of sin and salvation are also hammered flat on the anvil of praxis theory. To be sure, the salvation of the kingdom of God is not something that takes place merely in the hearts of people. No, there are social and political as well as personal and interior aspects of the kingdom of God, of eschatological salvation at work in history. But Christianity has learned not to expect too much from people who get up a big head of steam in the interest of saving the whole world by their own partisan type of praxis. A theology of the cross debunks every ideology that claims that the original sin that infects all humanity will be removed as a result of structural changes in the world wrought by human praxis. The redemptive energies of God do work in history to make changes also of a structural kind, but these changes do not remove the roots of sin in the infrastructure of human life. Similarly, Christianity teaches that in the midst of woeful social injustice and brutality, it is possible for a conversion to take place in the inner person and thus realize a redemption unmatched by changes in the objective social situation. The cross of Christ is a symbol of hope in the darkest hour of human suffering.

Liberation theology is so oriented to the theme of social praxis, which deals with the world we can do something about, that it neglects the theme of the individual person *coram deo,* which deals with a condition one can do nothing about. Suppose we postulate the victory of Marxist orthopraxis. Then we will have gained a liberated society not marked by injustice, inequality, poverty, oppression, and disease. Yet, this does not remove the question of the person *qua* person standing before the ultimate judgment of God. If a person is vexed by problems of anxiety, guilt, sin, death, and meaninglessness, the wonderful announcement that all elements of repression and violence have been removed from society would hardly bring the needed cheer to such a wretched soul. Kierkegaard would still be bent low by angst in a Marxist classless paradise.

Liberation theology runs the risk of becoming merely the ideology of the socialist left in North Atlantic countries. This does not mean that Karl Marx's theory of praxis, revised by the Frankfurt school, is totally useless and unacceptable to Christian theology. However, since it is by no means a value-free concept, it needs to be criticized in light of the first principles of theology. The critical theory of praxis may have helped to expose hidden connections of traditional theology with the self-interest of ruling classes in society. Yet, its own analysis of society presupposes a prior commitment to the value of freedom as a transcendent absolute, and this enjoys a status above and beyond history, so to speak. For history itself is the history of unfreedom, or not-yet freedom.

The negative principle implied in liberating praxis is not contrary to the Christian spirit. The principle of negativity in fact is very much needed in Christian theology and is directly implied by a theology of the cross. However, this negative dialectic feeds on a prior positive source of meaning which has broken into history in Jesus Christ; the first task of theology is to understand this event before it calls for this or that kind of praxis. The relation between Christian theology and the critical theory of praxis is not one way, as though the latter alone stands to be revised and corrected. In fact, the traffic moves in both directions, so that the hermeneutical operations at work in Christian theology will be analyzed in light of the critical theory of society. Particularly, a critique of the ideological tendencies of theology and ecclesial praxis can work retroactively on a hermeneutical interpretation of Christian origins. This very usefulness of critical theory and praxis makes it all the more important to be vigilant of the possible mischief it can cause in theology while our guard is down.

In *Theology and the Philosophy of Science* Pannenberg makes clear in his discussion with the Frankfurt school, and Habermas' action-theory of knowledge in particular, that he cannot assign to praxis the status of priority. His argument here would apply as well to the way in which the liberation theologians hold to the Marxist concept of theory and praxis. For Pannenberg "the anticipation of meaning is always in one way or another constitutive of action."[20] A theory of action must presuppose the awareness of meaning as the more fundamental aspect of human life. The anticipation of the meaning of the world as a whole is the prius of the meaning of actions. This concern for the meaning of the world as a whole is the main theme of religion and theology. Pannenberg fears that along the line of Habermas' action-theory of knowledge (as well as liberation theology's definition of theology as a critical theory of praxis) truth can hardly be reached, because knowledge itself never becomes independent of its basis in biological instincts, material needs, and human interests. Pannenberg is here responding to Habermas' position expressed in *Knowledge and Human Interests*.

Pannenberg is more appreciative of Habermas' dialectical concept of the relation of parts and whole implied in all experience of meaning.[21] For Pannenberg, too, the category of totality is fundamental in his theory of meaning in history. In the structure of the perception of meaning the concept of totality is implicitly present as a prerequisite of perceiving anything meaningful at all. Pannenberg believes, however, that this aspect of Habermas' concept of meaning cannot be justified on the basis of Habermas' theory of action. "It is quite impossible to carry on 'life activity' except through the medium of the understanding of meaning."[22]

Habermas developed his own concept of meaning in relation to the social context of life. Pannenberg sides with Gadamer in arguing that this is insufficient.[23] Pannenberg states: "The totality of meaning as the universe of meaning experienced and implicit in experience also transcends society. Society is not the embodiment of all reality and meaning, but needs itself in its particular current form to be rooted in and corrected by an absolute confidence in meaning which can transcend both conflicts between individual and society and the tension between man and nature. This absolute confidence in meaning has historically been embodied in religions as the basis of particular social orders and also as the potential for their renewal."[24] It is this theme of the "whole" or "totality" in hermeneutical theory that provides a foothold for theology. Theology as a science of God claims as its special subject matter reality as a whole, even though this whole is incompletely reflected in language and experience. It is hard to see how the notion of the primacy and priority of society-transforming praxis, which is at best only one aspect of human life, can provide theology with its own specific theme, and not instead result in an *Aufhebung* of theology in favor of a particular social order.

The Priority of a Meaningful Vision

Although the stress on the priority of praxis in political and liberation theologies may be unacceptable to a theology that gives priority to the divine indicative in biblical revelation, it may still serve as a challenge to all static views of truth and reality. It may help to remind theology that the biblical view of truth and revelation is inextricably linked to an ongoing transformation of reality, one that is oriented to the future (eschatology) and guided by the promises of freedom. The symbols of the Christian faith are not meant to be gathered up into timeless, abstract propositional truths. They reveal what God is doing in the world to change it. The dictum of Karl Marx has almost a biblical ring: "The philosophers have only interpreted the world; but the point is to change it."

A theology of history oriented to social change is intrinsically related to the future and the changes that a vision of freedom calls for. The prime symbols of the faith do not only give us *new revelation* but point to the future of *new reality* for which God calls upon the church to spend itself in missionary service.

Christian theology must spell out its case clearly against the Marxist notion of the priority of praxis. The first point is that within the structure of a Christian theology, the kerygma about Jesus and the kingdom of God (the gospel) is the prius of every transformative praxis. Ethics stems from eschatology; ethical fruits derive from eschatological roots. The biblical vision of the kingdom of God announces the imperatives of freedom and calls for emancipatory praxis, but makes their realization contingent upon the priority of the gospel indicatives. "Become what you are—for Christ's sake!" Freedom is first born when a meaningful vision of new possibilities invades the conditions of slavery. Moses cried out to Pharaoh, "Let my people go," and only then did things begin to happen. Freedom is primarily a function of eschatological hope grounded in the future of divine promise. Praxis is a second step. The burning bush comes before the parting of the Red Sea. Theology must be true to the divine indicative before it gives expression to any human imperative. Otherwise we are faced with a legalization of Christian faith, whereby the kingdom of God generates no gospel, but only the new law of transformative praxis.

Liberation theologians, like the old pietists, attack a dead orthodoxy and promise new life with the notion of orthopraxis. Only now this notion of orthopraxis is transposed from the pietistic cult of personal holiness to the arena of social righteousness. Such a notion will stub its toe on the Pauline doctrine of the gospel. The notion of new human action presupposes the notion of new human being. Being precedes act in the Pauline scheme of things. The new image of human being that gives rise to new possibilities of praxis is bound up with the appearance of Jesus Christ in history. The new reality in Jesus the Christ is generative of new praxis through the Spirit and the church. Although Christian faith affirms that the new reality has become historically embodied in the Word made flesh, this is an event that can be grasped first of all through faith alone. Such a faith will be active in love, doing the will of God. But faith is the prius of love in action.

Faith lays hold of the promises of a real future whose essential freedom is the norm and the goal of praxis. Christian faith does not merely convict the world of its alienation; it does not merely call for its radical transformation. It begins by confessing what God has already done in the world before we get a lick of the action. There is a priority of divine praxis in a relation of nonidentity to what we are asked to do in the world. The ultimate freedom of the world is already present in the world on account of Jesus Christ, in spite of all appearances to the contrary. Transformative praxis can become at best the historical working out of the reconciliation that is already present and active in the world as a result of the saving work of Jesus Christ.

The call in political and liberation theologies for the priority of praxis is shot through with the spirit of the Epistle of James, where it is written, "You see that a person is justified by works and not by faith alone" (James 2:24, RSV adapted). James also could speak of "mere talk" and appeal for "real love" and "good works," but James is one of the marginal writings in the canon of the New Testament. Paul was the real activist among the apostles, driven out of town for turning the world upside down through "mere" words of preaching. For Paul, the divine indicatives grasped by faith alone are the prius of the actions people are asked to perform. If praxis refers to what humans do for liberation, then it is necessary first to grasp those conditions which are the ground of the new possibilities of changing people and their societies in light of the messianic events that bear the imprint of God's approaching kingdom. I think Paul would want us to have these things clear before we rush in too boldly with dreams and schemes to change the world for the better.

God's Preferential Option for the Poor

A praxis-oriented interpretation of the church's mission lays great stress on the idea of God's preferential option for the poor. The

WCC Melbourne Conference on Mission and Evangelism, 1980, elevated the biblical notion that God takes the side of the poor.[25] Jesus declared at the start of his ministry: "The Spirit of the Lord is upon me, because he has anointed me to preach good news to the poor" (Luke 4:18). The church, in following Jesus, is called to bring the good news of hope to the poor. But preaching is not enough. The poor cannot eat words, and the massive misery of the impoverished majority must be met by concrete deeds of a political kind. The good news of the kingdom, if it is really good news, must bring something more than the consolation of words. There must be a politics of the kingdom to translate the words into actions that strike at the roots of poverty and misery in the world. In the effort to politicize the church's thinking about evangelism, contemporary political and liberation theologies have attempted to anchor their socialistic interpretation of the causes of poverty and oppression in the politics of Jesus and the kingdom.

Can the attempt to fuse the biblical message with political praxis legitimate itself with reference to the political dimensions of Jesus' message and ministry? Many New Testament scholars have correctly pointed out that traditional Christianity has downplayed the political facts involved in the struggles of Jesus with the authorities. It began already with Luke having the Roman centurion say as a witness to the crucifixion, "Certainly this man was innocent" (Luke 23:47). By sacrificing the political significance of Jesus' words and actions, the church thereby purchases a state license to operate without being harrassed as a religion of subversion. Along this line, the picture of the historical Jesus has become spiritualized and his message interiorized, minus all political implications. Jesus is usually pictured as a very pious man kneeling in prayer and looking up, dwelling on the more hallowed things of the celestial hierarchy. Such a person's politics are no threat to the establishment, so why persecute those who follow a leader who has made himself a political eunuch for heaven's sake?

Political and liberation theologies have helped to redress a one-sided picture of Jesus enveloped by a misty cloud of docetic spirituality. But we still have some questions suggested by looking at the gospel sources. Even if we acknowledge that Jesus was not politically neutral, that he taught a message with some kind of political impact, is it a politics that has any practical value in the real world? Will it work in Congress or City Hall? Does not politics look for compromise solutions to problems that do not necessarily end with somebody's crucifixion and death? Was not the politics of Jesus so utterly strange that to use the word for his actions requires a thousand and one qualifications? If established Christianity can be faulted for having depoliticized the message of Jesus in its own ideological self-interest, to keep Christianity in cahoots with the authorities downtown, is there not now an equal danger on the side of politicizing the gospel, loading it with an ideology from the left? Professor Henry Cadbury of Harvard University wrote a book entitled, *The Peril of Modernizing Jesus*. Of course, every generation does it. The latest bizarre example is the bronze sculpture of a female crucifix—Christa! The modern rediscovery of the political elements in the Gospels is a healthy corrective. But there is still the peril of trying to extract too much political ideology from the kerygma, with the result that we pour into the Bible whatever bias moves our fancy at the moment. In the case of Jesus we are dealing with a kind of apocalyptic politics, absolutely *sui generis,* not from the right or the left or the middle. We are dealing with an eschatological politics that puts an end to politics. It places all our politics under the judgment of the cross—the instrument of God's politics.

It is notoriously true that every age, race, and class seemingly finds in the historical Jesus a mirror of its own image. The warning implied in Albert Schweitzer's *Quest of the Historical Jesus* is still valid. He documented the history of the scholarly attempt to rediscover the historical Jesus and found that most historians have produced a modernized picture of Jesus to fit their own moral and religious worldview. Today Jesus is being pictured around the world as one of the poor and oppressed, although he came from a blue-collar family and his dad belonged to the carpenter's union. Nevertheless, the gospel portrait of Jesus does not place him in a special relationship with the poor of Yahweh. Jesus did announce the coming of the kingdom to the poor first, not the rich; to sinners, not the righteous; and to other defenseless people, not those on top. Jesus' message of the kingdom was bound up with the destiny of the poor in a onesided way. He placed no special moral or religious requirement in the way of the kingdom's coming to the poor and oppressed. This point underscores the unconditional character of the kingdom as God's gift to those who have no special merits to boast about. The monergism of the kingdom is clear. There is no room for synergism here if the kingdom of God comes to the poor and to all others unable to meet the moral and religious conditions which the churches have made prerequisite to the reception of the gospel.

The idea of Jesus' special relation to the poor still leaves other nagging questions unanswered. When the gospel is preached and the kingdom comes, what do the poor have to be cheerful about? Despite all of Jesus' best intentions, in spite of all his deeds of mercy and signs of wonder, Jesus did not make a successful attack on the conditions of poverty in his time. And those who have followed the way of Jesus have not eradicated poverty in theirs. Jesus did not diagnose the cause of poverty; he did not discover a cure for misery and oppression—except for one thing! He promised the poor that, when the kingdom comes, things will be different. When God's kingdom comes —not when there is more social progress, nor with the next revolution! Jesus' message has a point of reference to the future, albeit the very near future. It is not the case that the poor are *already* happy in the presence of Jesus. As long as we have the poor with us, they are the sure sign of the absence of the kingdom. Poverty is not a blessed state. Poverty is not to be spiritualized and glamorized.

Christians are in a dilemma. They believe that the kingdom has come already in Jesus, yet the fact of massive poverty is proof of its absence. Jesus' promise of happy days for the poor never came true in his time nor at any time since. Jesus seems to have promised the poor more than they have ever got. The kingdom did not come as expected. According to the New Testament, the kingdom has come in Jesus, hidden under the cross and the resurrection. Meanwhile, that kingdom has not come with all power and glory to put an end to the real sufferings, the horrible brutalities, and the grinding poverty in which milllions of people have had to exist through no fault of their own.

The delay of the kingdom is a source of frustration. Why is God taking his time? Why do the poor have to wait so long? How long, O Lord, how long? No wonder some Christians have been seduced by the Marxist revival of the way of the Zealots. We can bring in the kingdom now by our revolutionary praxis. Perhaps in our time we can bring in the kingdom and fulfill Jesus' promise to the poor by some kind of political praxis, creating a new international order in which the rich nations will experience their comeuppance and the poor nations will be showered with blessings. But what we have instead are more megatrends giving us more and more of 1984.

The early Christians did not give us a picture of the world made new and free of poverty by the coming of the kingdom. They gave us the story of a man crushed by the powers of the old world and made new by the miracle of the resurrection. The early church interpreted Jesus' expectation of the kingdom as fulfilled in his cross and resurrection, not in the elimination of poverty. In fact, the redactor in Matthew, for example, changed the "Q" source from "Blessed are the poor" to "Blessed are the poor in spirit" (Matt. 5:3), referring not to the really poor but to humble Christians. This was an adjustment made after Easter, taking due account of the postponement of the parousia. The fulfillment of the kingdom is hidden in the person of Jesus, while the emaciated bodies of the poor line the streets of Calcutta and wither away under the sun of the sub-Sahara. The crucified Christ is the embodiment of the kingdom in its hiddenness under the conditions of misery in this world. We have a message of the suffering Christ to preach to the world, but in all honesty neither we nor anyone else has come up with a real solution to the problem of poverty. Such a Christology can affirm his solidarity with all the poor, all the beggars, all the oppressed of history. It is a solidarity that calls for Christians to act in favor of the poor at all times. Such a Christology enlists churches to become advocates and partisans in the struggles of the poor, to try to loosen the grip of the powers of domination on the lives of the poor. But Christians would be guilty of oversell if they claimed that the gospel they preach and the praxis it engenders will provide social, political, and economic remedies to the ills that afflict humankind.

The Socialist Way to the Kingdom

We have raised numerous questions about the place of praxis in Christian theology. Our response to these questions has been dialectical, consisting of both yes and no. In some Christian circles to the left, there is no toleration of the no. "Either you are with us or you are against us." I believe we need to hear the critical voices of those who say no, especially when we have begun to espouse a new way of thinking.

Wolfhart Pannenberg has looked down the road to which liberation theology is pointing and passionately rejects not only its theory of praxis but the very socialistic way to which liberation theology is committed. In a heated exchange with Helmut Gollwitzer, Pannenberg has explained his opposition to any alliance of Christian theology with socialism.[26] Theologians on the left are attracted to the socialist vision of a society built on the principles of freedom and justice, a society in which no group or class is dominated and oppressed by others. These broad social ideals, however, are rooted in the tradition of liberal democracy, and are by no means special to socialism. Actually, the original roots of these liberal social ideals come from the the Stoic concept of human nature, which Christianity in turn fused with its own biblical vision of the kingdom of God, heralding peace and righteousness. The authentic Christian hope that the coming rule of God will overcome the situation in which some people are impoverished, humiliated, and dominated by a ruling class does not mean that Christians must be socialists today. The issue before us is not the merit of the ideals of freedom and justice. These are principles which both socialistic and liberal ideologies share. The issue for Pannenberg is, rather, the *way* in which we go about reaching these goals or implementing these values. He does not accept the socialist way or the assumption of the Christian left that Christianity can bind the integrity of its faith and hope to one particular praxis.

Thus, not the socialist ideal but the socialist way is the direct target of Pannenberg's break with the Christian left. Pannenberg understands the socialist way to call for an end to the private ownership of the means of production as the way to bring about the true freedom of every individual. The underlying premise consists of an optimistic view of human nature, contradicting the biblical estimate that sin and evil lie deep in the infrastructure of every person, so that individuals by nature are more interested in seeking their own freedom at the expense of others than in pursuing the rational insight that the well-being of each is somehow dependent on the realization of the common good. This deep tendency of persons to secure their own freedom at the cost of others is not exclusively manifest in a system of private ownership, but expresses itself with equal vigor in striving for power, influence, and fame.

The tragedy of modern socialism is that the socialist revolutions and the socialization of the means of production have not generated a consensus of individuals free of coerciveness. Many excuses are made for this delay in the realization of true freedom, while the interim period in which coercion is required becomes indefinitely prolonged. In every case, some particular group assumes the competence to decide what is in the true interest of all and what sacrifices individuals must make to bring about the socialist aims. It is no accident, Pannenberg claims, that wherever the socialist revolution has been successful, this has led to some of the most enslaving political conditions known to humanity in modern times. This is not due to any unfortunate set of circumstances which could in principle be rectified next time. Rather, we are faced here with a basically false doctrine of human nature embedded in the foundations of socialist theory. Nor can the socialists of today be pardoned on the grounds of naiveté, not after so many socialist revolutions have invariably produced totalitarian systems of domination. There are virtually no empirical grounds to support the promises of socialism. On the contrary, the facts of historical experience contradict them.

Christian faith lives in the expectation of the kingdom of God as a coming rule of peace and righteousness, which will definitively put an end to our human systems of domination and oppression. But there is no causal connection between the socialist plan to get rid of the private ownership of the means of production and the coming of God's kingdom. Christians do not have the duty to be socialists for the kingdom's sake.

The Christian hope for the kingdom of God is deeply suspicious of every political scheme to inaugurate a world of peace and justice. Only God will bring in such a new world, not the overthrow of a system of private ownership of the means of production. This does not mean that God's rule of peace and righteousness is thoroughly otherworldy, something only for the next life. The real presence of this eschatological kingdom has been embodied in the Christ event and is signaled by those who receive his rule through faith and hope. This is, of course, precisely what Marxists and socialists (including some liberation theologians) recognize as a kind of religious opiate. However, Pannenberg will not be put on the defensive. He is mounting an offensive against the socialist superstition that the realization of true humanity will be established as a direct consequence of the elimination of the private ownership of the means of production, as though this is the sole or even the chief obstacle to the flowering of the goodness of human nature. This superstition is no harmless illusion. In our century it has been combined with the kind of political fanaticism that has offered up the lives of millions of people on the altar of socialism, without having succeeded in minimizing in the least the domination of the many by the few. Slavery and oppression continue under socialism in new and different forms, and cannot be justified as mere "functional subordination" (Gollwitzer's term). Instead of pushing Christians toward the socialist option, Pannenberg believes that theologians would do better to remember the realistic anthropology of the Bible and dispel the superstition that something like the kingdom of God, with its promise of peace and freedom, justice and righteousness, can be brought about by the socialist revolution.

The alliance of liberation theology with socialism in the Marxist sense accounts for a good deal of the kind of religious rhetoric we find in liberation theology. The idea of a partisan God is particularly odious to Pannenberg. The Bible warns every group against the tendency to recruit God for our holy crusades, even if this be a socialist crusade claiming to represent the interests of the oppressed against the self-interest of the oppressors. The temptation is strong to recruit God for any cause that calls itself "liberationist" and to announce his blessing on the prejudices that stem from that cause.

One such prejudice, Pannenberg feels, is the widespread notion that "the poverty of some is the necessary consequence of the affluence of others. The prejudice ignores numerous economic and social realities, but it does have the almost irresistible merit of simplicity."[27]

Pannenberg states: "The Bible knows nothing about a partisan God."[28] This runs counter to one of the chief refrains in liberation theology. Pannenberg means that God does not side with the self-interest of any party. He cannot be claimed for one side in any struggle between people. The God of the Bible is no respecter of persons. The kingdom comes to establish the righteousness of God, which can be taken as the foundation of the rights of human beings, but these rights cannot be exchanged for egoistic self-interests.

Here is a powerful quotation to ponder: "Talk about a partisan God should immediately remind us of the opposing armies of Christians going to war under the banner, 'God With Us.' In such a confrontation, there can indeed be no *common* Christian hope. Our hope is in a righteousness that is radically independent of our self-interested causes. Further, the gospel makes clear that we only participate in that righteousness as we seek reconciliation with others, especially our enemies. Not taking sides, but reconciliation, is the Christian answer. The hope speaks not of partisanship but of repentance on the part of all."[29]

Pannenberg's attack on socialism as the way to the kingdom of God is addressing the situation in West Germany, where an elite group of intellectuals are romantically embracing ideals of Marxist socialism, without learning any lessons from its monstrous distortions in Russia and its military enslavement of the Eastern bloc of European nations. The Christian left is mouthing Marxist slogans, seemingly blind to the clear consequences to which they have led. There are other forms of socialism that would not merit the sharp critique of Pannenberg, forms of democratic socialism in West European countries. In these countries socialism has not led to the extinction of freedom in the classical liberal sense.

PART THREE:
A Ministry for Mission

7

The Apostolic Foundations
of Ministry

The Precarious State of the Ministry Today

The promise of renewal of the church's mission depends on the recovery of the apostolic ministry in the church today. Every church, denomination, and sect has laid claim to a ministry which in all essentials is apostolic. They all profess that their ministries stand in apostolic succession. That is because every kind of Christian community lives or dies by its ability to transmit the true apostolic stuff, whatever that is. But they seem to contradict each other.

On a spectrum from left to right, left-wing Protestants have a vague sense of *spiritual* continuity with the first Christians. The continuity is not mediated through any doctrine or creed, cult or ritual, symbols or sacraments, offices or authorities. It just happens by spontaneous combustion in a spiritual sort of way through the inner life. This kind of mysticism often peters out into a weak imitation of the *ecclesia apostolica*. In the middle are those who stress continuity with apostolic doctrine. It is the orthodox model that works fiercely to eliminate all heresy from the body. To its credit, it keeps alive the memories of the creeds and confessions of the classical epochs of the Christian tradition. But it often becomes overly rigid in its zeal to conserve unaltered the traditions of the past and paranoid about modernity and new things. Further to the right are those who would go beyond doctrinal continuity and include the ministerial office. But churches do not agree on the nature of this office, though most today admit that some kind of office is necessary. Lutherans have said that only the office of ministering to the word and sacraments is essential. To the right of that are Catholics and Orthodox who require a collegial succession of bishops, and still further to the right are Roman Catholics who place the pope at the head of the church and all its ministries. This plurality of convictions about what is authentic apostolicity in the church today poses the greatest ecumenical challenge. But this ecumenical fact of pluralism is only one aspect of the problem of ministry today.

The crisis of ministry has many root causes. Ministers properly ordained according to the rubrics of their own denominations are experiencing identity crisis and burnout. This malaise cannot be attributed to the ecumenical dimension of the problem. It lies deeper in the heart of the minister's faith and call. Regardless of doctrine, high church or low church, from the Protestant left to the Catholic right, priests and pastors do not know who they are or what they are supposed to be doing. Many have simply dropped out and looked for another vocation. Males have been losing interest in preparation for ordained ministry, not only in the Catholic church with its obligatory celibacy, but also in Protestant communities, which fortunately have recently opened the doors to women. Many seminaries now count almost 50% women studying for ordination. To some this poses a doctrinal problem, to others an administrative problem, but we still have to ask, where have all the men gone? The crisis facing the Roman Catholic church is reaching major proportions, and is deeply symptomatic of the problem of ministry today.[1]

Even with a robust sense of calling, wherein one's personal confidence of an "inner call" is wonderfully confirmed by the church's "public call" to the special ministry, there are innumerable problems. The special ministry is less than 1% of the total membership of the church. The minister is like a cook serving up meals to customers. Ministers often feel they are the only ones doing ministry. The attitude among many laity is, they are paid for it, let them do it! The special ministry has to work overtime because the general ministry of all believers has been put to sleep. This is a structural problem complicated by centuries of sociological history. As the minister carries out the entire work of ministry, the minister must become a jack of all trades, an amateur functioning in many fields in which people want experts.

In the New Testament there was a fantastic plurality of ministries and gifts of service generously distributed among the baptized. Through the process of historical development, many of these roles and functions collapsed into the one office of the local leader. Ideally, that person needs to be omnicompetent. The crisis of ministry has revealed the weakness of the system, compared with the more open, flexible, and multiple patterns of ministry in primitive Christianity. The minister today is expected to be a good shepherd, expert in pastoral care and counseling; to preside at the liturgy, preaching the Word and administering the sacraments in an inspiring and challenging manner; to reach out into the community, ringing doorbells and building the membership; to bring the prophetic witness of the gospel into the larger society, acting in behalf of its most unfortunate victims; to keep up his or her own piety and spirituality, always a source of consolation and joy to others. The personal qualities and skills needed to fulfill all these roles in a competent way are more than most ministers possess. In New Testament times it would have been unthinkable that all of these roles and functions would have devolved on one person in the congregation. We are victims of a monomorphic system of ordained leadership. It is a weak system and the mission of the church is being short-circuited.

But the problem of ministry runs deeper. We have touched on the *ecumenical* and *systemic* dimensions of the crisis. There is also a *theological* root. Trends that began in the Enlightenment have worked their way into the collective Christian consciousness—rationalism, naturalism, materialism, secularism, nihilism, and what not. Before a person is five years into the ministry—or perhaps it happens all the way through the years of preparation for ministry—there are the nagging questions and corrosive doubts that sap the energies of commitment, discipleship, and sacrifice. Is there anything distinctive about the call to the special ministry of the church?

Is the only difference between clergy and laity that some are dressed up in ecclesiastical garb and get paid for it? Is there anything more than a purely functional reason for the ordained ministry, putting the ministry on a par with other professions, the mandate coming from the community, not from the Lord—that is "from below" and not "from above"? Does anything supernatural happen at ordination? Does it bestow some "indelible character," a permanent charism? Was it really instituted by Christ and perpetuated by his Spirit through prayer and the laying on of hands, beginning with the apostles? Does the ministry of Word and sacraments really convey the gifts of eternal life under the conditions of historical existence, or is it rather a means to liberate people from their hang-ups, for the realization of their human potential, or to overcome social systems that alienate and oppress? Could one perhaps make an impact more directly on the problems that afflict people today through psychological counseling or social action?

Joseph Sittler was one of the first to detect the symptoms of the emerging crisis in ministry. In 1959, he wrote a pioneering article for *The Christian Century* entitled, "The Maceration of the Minister."[2] Maceration means "to chop up into small pieces." Seminaries teach what the ministry is supposed to mean in idealistic terms, but the actual practice of ministry chops it to pieces. Whatever the talk about Word and sacraments, gospel and salvation, the chief role of the minister is to further the external advancement of the congregation, securing a growing membership roll, higher annual budgets, a new and finer sanctuary, all to the glory of First Lutheran on Main Street. "It is hard for the minister to maintain a clear vision of who he is when he is so seldom doing what he ought."[3] (There were only male ministers at that time.)

The stampede for relevance brought the ministry to the top of the pinnacle, and it has come crashing down. In the 1980 report and analysis on *Ministry in America,* edited by Davis S. Schuller, Merton P. Strommen, and Milo L. Brekke, David Schuller writes about the various ways in which ministers have sought to retain relevance in ministry while coping with their doubts and frustrations. One group found confidence in a return to biblical fundamentals. "This group's response to a future that might overwhelm them was to turn to the past for scriptural and theological anchors that might keep them from being swept away."[4] Another group, far to the left, worked for the professionalizing of the ministry, using the medical and legal professions as models. Draw up a list of competences, provide a set of skills, create the means of measuring accountability, and you have the makings of a profession.

Neither of these two approaches has solved the problem of ministry. The approach of returning to the past for secure models, to Scripture and tradition, has been rendered extremely problematic by the relativizing impact of historical-critical research. What are the biblical fundamentals? How did things get started and go forward? What developments are appropriate? Can we really draw a faithful trajectory anchored in the ministry of Jesus and the witness of the apostles? In the past each tradition—Orthodox, Roman Catholic, Calvinist, Anglican, Lutheran, Congregational, and Pentecostal has found its own kind of ministry fully supported in the New Testament. Modern critical-historical research has pulled the rug out from under all of them, so that the appeal of official church commissions to return to the biblical basics seems to lack a solid foundation. Roman Catholic scholars now concede that no form of ministry like that of pope, bishop, or priest can be found in the New Testament. The New Testament does not even have a word for pope or priest. As Raymond Brown, one of the most respected Roman Catholic New Testament scholars, has strikingly stated, "No individual Christian is ever specifically identifed as a priest."[5] Jesus is called a priest, and the church as a whole is called a royal priesthood, but there was no particular group of priests in the New Testament church. Nor was there anything like a special class of ordained persons presiding at the Eucharist as their special prerogative. Nor was the Eucharist originally thought of as a sacrifice which would require a special class of priests. Nor is there an unbroken chain of links connecting today's bishops with Peter and the other apostles.[6]

It is not only the Roman Catholic doctrine of ministry that is hit hard by contemporary findings of research into early Christian origins. The attempt of the Protestant Reformers, particularly in the Calvinist line, to restore the order of things as they were in the New Testament church has proved to be equally unsuccessful. Calvin believed that in shaking off the yoke of repressive order and authoritarian discipline of the medieval hierarchical system, it was possible to reestablish the mode of government in the church delivered to us in Scripture.[7] He called for a church order with four offices: pastors, teachers, elders, and deacons. That Calvin's genius was able to create such an order proved to be a stroke of good fortune for his heirs. Lutherans were not so lucky. Calvinists have been blessed with a book of order, Lutherans with a book of confessions. Lutherans have consequently looked like a bunch of ecclesiological docetists to Calvinists, lacking the ecclesial order to give expression to its evangelical faith. Lutherans have insisted on the *"satis est"* principle, namely, that for the unity of the church "it is enough" to agree on the true preaching of the word and the right administration of the sacraments. But Calvinists have retorted, *"Satis est non satis est,"* and some contemporary Lutherans are beginning to agree.

In addition to the apostolic gospel, the church must have an apostolic ministry. As the gospel must be normatively interpreted by creeds and confessions, so also the ministry must be effectively ordered by offices and functions. But the assumption that we can find such an order for the church in the givens of Scripture has been exploded by historical research. Not only can no church find its way of ordering the ministry mandated by Scripture, but also we find patterns of ministry in the New Testament which can be found as such in none of the churches in our day.[8] No church can claim to be in the right; no church can credibly claim that its ministry embodies the New Testament forms. What we find here and there in the New Testament communities is an irretrievable number of ministries: apostles, teachers, evangelists, miracle workers, pastors, leaders, bishops, helpers, prophets, elders, deacons, exorcists, faith healers, glossalaliasts, administrators, and others. The only constant, it seems, is the common Word and Spirit from which they all devolve, around which they all revolve.

We have shown that the return to a golden age of biblical precedents does not so easily resolve the disputes about ministry today. In the light of historical research new questions are raised that make the problem more acute. But the approach to the crisis at the other end of the spectrum, the professionalizing of the ministry, has contributed to its further secularization, and the last state becomes worse than the first. In the midst of uncertainty about the precise role of ministers in church and society, the professionalist approach focuses on tangible goals. In recent years ministers have been trained to become counselors, working in small groups or one on one. Their response to the crisis of ministry is to become a ministry of crisis, and there are always enough disturbed people who cannot afford the high fees of psychiatrists and psychologists to keep ministers busy.

Deeper analysis has shown that the "voice of illness" is a symptom of deep social pathology. When individuals become sick, they are giving voice to profound systemic wrongs. It is not good enough to change individuals; society itself must be changed. Many ministers since the roaring sixties think of themselves as change-agents. What's the use of preaching and counseling when our struggle is against the demons of nuclear war, pollution, overpopulation, poverty, unemployment, injustice, racism, classism, sexism, etc.? Some clergy who move in this direction have adopted a pseudo-Marxist liberationist ideology, which intensifies their rhetoric and radicalizes their stance. So far this approach has failed to find the political muscle to make any basic societal changes for the better. Quite a few who threw themselves into radical politics for a spell have reversed themselves and have followed the trail into the inner life, exploring everything from Jungian gnosticism to Zen spirituality. None of these experiments in ministry has scored mighty victories for the gospel of Christ and God's mission to the world by apostolic standards. As responses to the crisis of ministry, they have carried it further away from its appointed apostolic purpose. The deadly serious question is whether we can get the ministry back on track by discovering what makes ministry apostolic and essentially Christian. There can be no other resolution of the crisis of identity than to root the ministry in the divine election of the church to be the sacrament of the gospel of Christ's kingdom and to recognize that it is the nature of the ministry to be the instrument of the gospel's mission to the church and the world. This sacramental view of the church coupled with an instrumental view of its ministry may do justice to both the vertical and horizontal aspects of the doctrine of ministry. The ministry of the church will be seen as coming vertically from above, linked to the salvation events in the word of Christ and the witness of the apostles, as well as developing horizontally from below through a plurality of forms of service in changing historical situations. We have the treasures of ministry in earthen vessels. There is no *logos* without *sarx,* no spirit without letter, no gospel without church, and no mission without ministry. It is always the gnostic-docetic heresy that separates what God has joined together in the foundational events of two incarnations—first, the Word made flesh in Jesus and second, his gospel becoming history through the once-for-all apostolic witness and its continuing succession through the church as a whole and through an evolving plurality of ministries of service. Our so-called special ministry of Word and sacraments, or the threefold office of ministry of pastor, bishop, and deacon, must be derived from these foundational events and verified with reference to the question: Do they preach Christ aright? Do they help or hinder the gospel's mission in the church and to the world? This is the call of the Reformation. It must be re-sounded in the present ecumenical search for an ordered ministry that serves the gospel of Christ and his church's mission to the world.

The Authority of Christ and the Apostles

God in Christ has reconciled us to himself and has given us the ministry of reconciliation (2 Cor. 5:18). Human beings are not able to free themselves from sin and guilt and to reconcile themselves to God through any sacrifice or works of their own. The total ministry of Jesus Christ, his sermons, parables, miracles, and actions, as well as his death on the cross and his resurrection from the dead, was God's way of reconciling the world to himself. This constitutes the central message of the ministry of reconciliation which God has entrusted to the church (2 Cor. 5:19).

The entire theme of ministry in the New Testament is bound to the person of Jesus Christ as the decisive eschatological event of God's reconciling Word. Christ alone is the unity in, with, and under the pluriformity of ministries that arose in primitive Christianity. Ministry is Christocentric in all the New Testament writings, before anything else can be said about it. This does not mean that it is not at the same time trinitarian, for the ministry of reconciliation is the gift of the Holy Spirit empowering the church with various charisms for building up the community. If there is any authority in the church, the source of such authority can be none other than Jesus Christ, as that authority is mediated through those whom he commissioned to be his ambassadors. The Christological titles of the New Testament underscore the sole authority of Jesus Christ in the church. He is the "Lord," "Son of God," "Savior," "high priest." These titles identify Jesus Christ as the author of salvation, the way, the truth, and the life. The personal authority of Jesus Christ is the point of departure for the doctrine of the church and its ministry.

The ministry began with Jesus Christ. He had his ministry from the Father who sent him on a far journey, and he chose a select few to go into the world as his representatives. This is a ministry which comes from above, as the apostle Paul understood it. "Paul an apostle—not from men nor through man, but through Jesus Christ and God the Father, who raised him from the dead" (Gal. 1:1). In these words Paul is attacking the notion that he has received his calling as an apostle from the consent of the people, in a democratic way. The risen Christ called and appointed him to be an apostle-missionary, even before he was born (Gal. 1:15). It is clear that an apostle is not self-selected or democratically elected to his office in the church. It is Christ who calls and sends the apostle. This is the sovereign action that places the whole church on the foundation of the apostles, with Jesus Christ being the chief cornerstone (Eph. 2:20). The church is founded on the apostles, and the apostles are founded on Jesus Christ. "For no other foundation can anyone lay than that which is laid, which is Jesus Christ" (1 Cor. 3:11).

With Christ as its prime paradigm the ministry is radically determined to be a kind of service. Ministry is service. It began with Christ Jesus himself, who took the form of a servant (Phil. 2:7), who "came not to be served but to serve, and to give his life as a ransom for many" (Mark 10:45). From this it follows that the person in the church "who is greatest among you shall be your servant" (Matt. 23:11). Every claim to overlordship is to be repudiated. Every system based on rank in a hierarchical pyramid of powers does not belong in the church of Christ. "What then is Apollos? What is Paul? Servants through whom you believed, as the Lord assigned to each" (1 Cor. 3:5). Anyone who bears the office of ministry owes a double loyalty of service, first to the Lord, and then to the community.

It is clear that in the earliest New Testament community the apostles were the first appointed (1 Cor. 12:28). Next came prophets, then teachers, miracle workers, healers, etc. Who were these first apostles without whose witness we would know nothing about Jesus Christ and his saving benefits? They had their authority from Jesus Christ, and we derive ours ultimately through them. We confess that the church is apostolic; we intend to say that it exists in continuity with the apostles and their proclamation of Jesus Christ. Contemporary New Testament scholarship has clarified the distinction between the twelve disciples and the apostles. Jesus chose twelve disciples from among his followers and even sent them forth on preaching missions. But it was the resurrection that constituted the apostolate. When the Gospels refer to the Twelve as apostles, they are placing the mantle of the postresurrection apostles on the shoulders of the disciples. It was only as witnesses to the risen Lord that Peter and the other disciples become foundation stones of the church. The paradigm of the apostle was Paul, and he was never a disciple of Jesus. But Peter, who was a disciple, was also a ranking apostle— the first witness of the risen Christ. The link of the apostolate to the resurrection of Jesus is the key to its place of authority in the young church.

The apostolate comes before the church. Foundations must be laid before a house can be built. The apostles received their authority directly from Christ; they were commissioned to be his messengers and ambassadors endowed with Christ's own authority. "He who receives you receives me" (Matt. 10:40). "He who hears you hears me" (Luke 10:16). It is absolutely crucial for the contemporary church to overcome its own crisis of authority by starting with the foundations of apostolic authority in the church, because that authority came directly from Jesus Christ. The answer to the question of what is authentic and authoritative in the church is purely and simply what is apostolic. Who were the apostles and what did they do that theirs should be the last word in the church? They were missionaries in the broadest sense of the word, founders of believing communities. Preaching was at the core of their assignment. There were no apostles who were not also missionaries. A church has a right to call itself apostolic only if it carries on the work of the apostles—going into all the world in order to make disciples in all the nations by teaching and baptizing. We do not know the names of the first apostles, except for Paul, Peter, James, and a few others. But we have summaries of their witness in the texts of the New Testament. We can be apostolic today only by renewing our relationship with their testimonies. These testimonies have a special authority for all time. The position and authority of the apostles are unique, once-for-all, and unrepeatable in later generations. After the first generation there could be no successors to the apostles. Paul was the last apostle. When they all died, the foundational period of the building up of the church came to an end. The last chapter in the definitive revelation of God's will and testament to the nations came to an end. There could never be a supplement, on the same level of authority, to the gospel the apostles preached. Just as there would never have to be another Messiah, another incarnation of the Son of God, another crucifixion for the salvation of the world, another resurrection of the crucified Christ, so also there would never have to be another set of apostles, another set of primary witnesses to the risen Lord, another foundational period in the history of the church. The apostolate is part of the once-for-all character of the events and interpretations that make up the original gospel.

When the apostles died, what would have to happen to keep the church apostolic in changing times? The apostolic word and witness would have to be passed on. Passing it on is the meaning of tradition. But not everything that got passed on from the time of the apostles was good stuff. Distortions and constrictions could and did enter in right from the beginning. However, what is true and what is false in the developing traditions of the church in postapostolic times is one of the most tangled issues of contemporary theology. Exegetes and dogmaticians do not agree on the matter. Broadly speaking, there are two lines of interpretation. The radical Protestant line holds that the only true and trustworthy form of tradition that we have is the word and witness of the apostles written down in the canon of the New Testament. The great Heidelberg professor of ecclesiastical history, Hans von Campenhausen, wrote a book that has been extremely influential in Protestant circles, *Ecclesiastical Authority and Spiritual Power in the Church of the First Three Centuries*. He says, "The once-for-all character of the apostolic calling is completely incompatible with the idea of an organized office, the essence of which is that it remains constant even when the holders change. The apostles, who had been called by name, found, as we saw, no successors."[9] According to von Campenhausen, there was no such thing as an apostolic office left vacant when an apostle died, which would have to be filled by a successor. There were no successors of the apostles, just as there were no successors of Christ. Nevertheless, apostolic authority continues in the life of the church in the form of the canon. "It was the latter [the New Testament canon] which in a certain sense became the heir of the apostles' authority."[10]

In this Protestant view, the *only* channel of apostolic succession in the church is through the proclamation of the apostolic message. From the Catholic point of view apostolic authority is channeled not only through the canon but through an apostolic chain of magisterial office holders. The *office* itself continues and is filled by successors to the apostles, who are called bishops. The episcopal office is seen as an essential form of continuing apostolic authority in the church. It began already in the New Testament, documented particularly in the Pastoral Epistles, where we are told about how Timothy received his charism through the laying on of hands. This interpretation sees in this rite the bridge from apostolic authority in the primitive church to the monarchical episcopacy of early Catholicism.

Are these two views mutually incompatible, or are they both right in a certain sense? The Protestant view is too narrow, but its stress on the canon as the norm of what is truly apostolic in later times is correct. But the church is not a school of scribes and scholastics poring over the scrolls of Scripture. The church lives from the continuation of the apostolic ministry in order to preach good news, to teach and baptize, to share the Lord's Supper, and to lead the ministries of all the faithful. This is a ministry that continued from the beginning in undisrupted continuity with the missionary work of the apostles. There never was a church that had to start over from scratch without the prior initiative of the kind of ministering the apostles began. Just as preaching was the essential work of the apostles, an immediate reflex of the command of the risen Lord to go and tell the gospel to the nations, so also preaching the Word and witness of the apostles is the essence of apostolic succession in the history of the church. The apostles indeed had no successors. There are no apostles in the church today. Bishops are not successors of the apostles, nor are any others. The apostles are the foundation stones, and they enjoy a unique and unrepeatable place in the temple which the Spirit builds. By the same token, there is no church, properly speaking, that does not in some way live from apostolic transmission.

How is the once-for-all apostolic ministry carried out in the church today? The Protestant left tends to suggest that it happens in an undifferentiated way through all Christians, taking its stand on the premise of the priesthood of all believers. There is truth in this line, for indeed all the baptized are commissioned to participate in the ministry of proclamation, bearing witness to the mighty acts of God. However, just as Christ chose a handful of disciples out of all his followers, and just as only some became witnesses to the resurrection of Jesus and were thereby commissioned to be his apostles, so also, after the apostles, the special task of doing what they started was bestowed on particular persons "through prayer and the laying on of hands."

The Protestant line by itself cannot succeed. As a corrective of the sacredotal-cultic and legal-hierarchical captivity of the church in its medieval development, its critique is justified. But the church cannot live from a corrective. A person with a headache may need to take a pill, but the body cannot live on pills alone. Paul Tillich distinguished the "Protestant principle" from "Catholic substance"; the distinction is apropos in this regard. A Protestant negation of the Catholic development has led to a thoroughly secularized, functional, managerial, democratic concept of ministry in the church, bringing about a great reduction of the substantive catholic and apostolic tradition. No good can come of it. The secularized edition of the Protestant critique views the church as a group of individuals banding together out of similar spiritual experiences, forming local congregations. The congregations in turn band together to form a larger group, and so on, until you have the sum total of all Christians and congregations united by a common bureaucracy. This is called democracy in the church; it is run by big wheels who have been elected by the people and by little wheels who have been selected by a bureaucratically arranged and manipulated quota system. In this scheme, the reality of the church originates in the subjectivity of the individual, and then is built up from below, so to speak, from the local to the universal church. The idea of the universal church is seen as a pure abstraction, and the notion of apostolic authority mediated through Word and Spirit is held hostage to those who run the church on the model of secular politics.

Karl Barth believed that modern Protestantism was a heresy second only to Roman Catholicism. The one is the antithesis of the other. If Roman Catholicism started its thinking about the church and its ecclesiastical office from above, as a chain of hierarchical legal authorities reaching back to Christ and the apostles, the modern Protestant antithesis sees the office of the ministry as a product of enlightened democracy at work. Adolf von Harnack called it ''pneumatic democracy.'' The office or offices of ministry came into being when the congregations decided to parcel out certain jobs to various individuals. Office holders were appointed by the people to carry out their will, mostly for the sake of ''decency and order.'' Basically these officers are administrators, acting only on the authority delegated to them from the will of the people. Here the concept of apostolic authority in the church has fallen to its lowest abyss since the ancient gnostics claimed to have a hot line to the secrets of God.

When modern Protestantism surrenders the classical Reformation principle of the canon as the norm of apostolicity, and then puts the office of ministry at the mercy of the voting majority or of a coalition of delegates selected by a quota system, the basic links to apostolicity have been broken, and the end result is the apostate church of the counter-Christ.

The maintenance of the canon as the norm of apostolicity is essential for the church, and so is the office of the ministry that continues the primacy of the apostolic service of the Word to the whole community of Jesus Christ. The special office of the ministry of the

Word goes back to Jesus Christ through the apostles and derives its authority from theirs. This office is not derived from the community; it stems ultimately from Christ himself. The office is occupied by persons who have been appointed to the task in a manner that was practiced in the very earliest communities founded by the original apostles. Here lies the element of truth in the doctrine of apostolic succession, and it is also the key to the meaning of ordination. The priesthood of all believers is the *context* in which the apostolically derived office of ministry functions, but it is not the *basis* of that office. Ordained persons do not receive the authority of their ministry from their lay sisters and brothers. They receive personally through ordination the authority which Christ bestowed on his apostles, and which the apostles in turn passed on to those persons who would continue the apostolic gospel mission of founding and leading communities. However, lay persons have a right and a duty to test the pastoral exercise of that authority by the apostolic canon of Scripture. This provides the church with a system of checks and balances, so that authority will not degenerate into abusive power. As long as ministers faithfully proclaim the gospel, they stand not only *within* the community among the baptized members, but also *over against* the community as the representatives and messengers of Christ. They are appointed ambassadors of Christ in his stead, ministering with his authority.

There are thus two ways in which the voice of apostolic authority lives in the church: first, in the form of the New Testament canon, and second, in the office of ministry. Persons for this office are commissioned with the authority of Christ himself, missionaries and messengers at his command, servants of the Word and of all the hearers of the Word, shepherds of the flock, stewards of the mysteries of God in Word and sacraments, founders and leaders of new communities of faith. This is an office to which particular individuals are called and ordained. The New Testament apostle serves as the authoritative model of this office in the church until the day the Lord returns. But this office is bound to the apostolic word and witness transmitted by the New Testament canon. Its task is to continue to build up the church on the foundations which the apostles laid once for all time to come. This does not happen by having a

Bible lying around the house. The church is a "mouth house," said Luther. The apostolic legacy becomes a living voice in the church through the vicarious office of the ministry.

A Plurality of Ministries and Charisms

There was no monolithic ordering of the ministry in primitive Christianity. The apostles enjoyed a unique authority as the Lord's personal representatives, but they were surrounded and supported by the ministries and charisms of others. In the earliest stages of the Pauline communities there was no ecclesiastical office or particular church order. In addition to the authority of his own apostleship, he relied on a kind of charismatic constitution of the church, emphasizing the sovereignty of the Spirit, the freedom of all Christians to exercise their gifts, and a rejection of all human ordinances and authorities. But such a spontaneous, charismatic type of community could not sustain itself in the next generations, as the passing of time lengthened the distance from the apostolic beginnings, as heretical deviations emerged, as the numbers of converts increased, and as the glow of the Spirit began to fade. Thus there developed very rapidly a system of elders, modeled on the Jewish congregation, especially in Palestine. With this began the process of fusing "office" and "charism" in the embryonic church order that we can trace out in the Pastoral Epistles. There we begin to hear about bishops, presbyters, elders, and deacons, indicating that there was in each congregation a responsible cadre of leaders who had received official appointment. The charism of the Spirit was taken into the office and mediated through a ritual of prayer and the laying on of hands. A variety of types was eclectically assimilated and commingled in a developing church order which is often referred to as "early Catholicism."

It is a mistake to try to make an ecclesiological dogma out of the various models of office and ministry in the New Testament communities. It would be a mistake to play one model off against another, to try to get back to the free-wheeling spirituality of an early Pauline community or to elevate to normative status the catholic order in the Pastoral Epistles. The New Testament does not teach us how God wills to order the church and its ministry in a once-for-all way. What we get instead from the New Testament is a picture of beginnings and directions and stages of development, with no end in sight. It would be false to absolutize one of these stages, to try to replicate it in the church today, and to invest it with the authority of revelation. Equally dangerous would be to legitimate positivistically everything that came down the pike of history, to assume that whatever happened in structuring the church was supposed to have happened and must retain its validity for today. From the freedom of the early church to change and improvise, we can learn how to be open to new possibilities in ordering the church today, possibly even to return to earlier models that were never given much of a chance. Particularly the prophetic line of ministry needs to be revived in the church. We have bishops, pastors, and teachers, but where are the prophets? They are mentioned second only to the apostles. The church has so overreacted to false prophets, that it has become forever skeptical about there being true prophets. Prophets live in exile outside the institutional church.

What we have learned from the New Testament that is normative for ordering the ministry of the church today is the priority of Jesus Christ as God's gospel of reconciliation, and the authority of the apostolic witness as the keystone of the church's ministry. All other ministers, prophets, teachers, evangelists, pastors, bishops, elders, and deacons are radically dependent upon and derived from the special place of Christ and the apostles in the foundation of the church. There is no normative biblical church order into which they all fit. There is no old or new church polity that can be proved by citing biblical passages. But something is essential: the word and witness of the apostles must continue in the church, and there must be orderly ways of actualizing that witness. There may be no one particular way, but do it we must.

The church would not be living today if there had not been ways of continuing to do what the apostles had begun. In one sense the work of the apostles was finished; they laid the foundations. In another sense, it is still going on, for the command of Christ to "Go, tell it to the nations!" is in force until the end of time. When the church goes to the nations it is following in the footsteps of the apostles. The church maintains a true succession with the apostles along two tracks, the canon of Scripture and the office of ministry. The office of ministry has priority to the canon of Scripture, but the canon of Scripture holds the primacy.

There is a great deal of controversy in the church about how best to continue the apostolic thing going on in the church. The Roman Catholic church believes that bishops do it best, that the episcopal office is essential to its getting done at all. Bishops represent the apostles and exercise their authority in a special way. Protestant churches have countered with their stress on the canonical texts of Scripture. As someone has said, "Protestants have a paper pope." Since the Scriptures come from antiquity in a set of ancient languages, they must be translated and interpreted before they can be read and understood. Having lost the ministry of bishops in caring for the apostolicity of the church, Protestant churches, Lutheran and Calvinist, have relied heavily on theologians to perform the hermeneutical operations necessary to keep alive the memories of the apostolic Word and witness. Modern Protestants who have lost not only the episcopal connection but have also surrendered canonical authority have inevitably drifted into the fog of passing fads and fancies.

American Christianity has suffered such a great loss of apostolic substance that we have to ask whether we do not need a strategy of recovery on more than one front. Bishops are appointed to represent the apostolic office in the church in a special way. Theologians are called to interpret the canonical texts in relation to the changing contexts of later times. A healthy church needs the ministries of both bishops and theologians to strengthen the links to the apostolic heritage. Every church absolutely needs to have done what bishops exist to do, namely, to secure the right preaching and teaching of the gospel in the church, bound to the authority of the apostolic witness. The pastor of a local congregation is a bishop in this sense. As the church expanded, it discovered the need to develop the office of *episcopē* beyond the local level, as a sign and instrument of the one true apostolic church at the regional, national, and universal levels. Even the emergence of the papal office in the ancient church, apart from the later dogma about papal infallibility, can be accounted for along this line of development. As part of the expansion of the ministry of overseeing apostolic work in the church at every level, we can raise no theological objection to the papal office.

What about the ministry of theology? Its apostolic teaching function rests absolutely on the condition that it subordinate itself to the apostolic canon of Holy Scripture. That is, of course, not the case in wide circles of contemporary theology. Whatever else theologians find of interest to do, nothing can alter the fact that their only contact with the original witnesses to the foundational events on which the church stands is to be found in the Scriptures. Theologians can become again credible *doctores ecclesiae* only as servants of the church and teachers of the truth in the apostolic line that combines the authority of Jesus and the power of his Spirit. Bishops and theologians have different offices and charisms, but they are united as witnesses to the apostolically transmitted Word in the power of the Spirit, both of which go back to the authority of Jesus Christ.

This view of authority from the perspective of apostolic origins must relativize the whole succeeding development of official authority in the church. The better we grasp the beginnings of Christianity in all their historical and theological complexity, the less credible will be the self-aggrandizing claims attached to the traditional structures that have emerged in church history. Neither the authoritarian Catholic "right" nor the enthusiastic Protestant "left" can stand in face of the actual facts about authority and power in early Christianity. Yet, a great number of our ecumenical conversations proceed on their way, oblivious to this challenge coming from our historical knowledge of Christian origins.

The issue of official authority is concerned for the right ordering of the church. But the church does not exist to serve the clergy, but vice versa. The power of the Spirit cannot be confined to any of the offices in the church. The tendency arose early in the church for its officeholders to claim control over the charisms of the Spirit. But in Baptism all the *laos* are ordained by the Spirit and empowered by the gifts of the Spirit. The spiritual authority and power embodied in Christ and his apostles cannot be monopolized by the established offices of the church, because there are charismatic powers liberally conferred on all believers. Sometimes the tension between official authority and charismatic power reaches the breaking point. The ordained leaders can become false prophets, theologians can become heretics, bishops can become tyrants and, when this happens, congregations may be led by unordained charismatic leaders in a movement of protest and dissent. Free-church traditions remind the rest of us that all the properly constituted offices in the church do not guarantee true succession in the apostolic line. The Spirit blows where and when it wills, and cannot be confined to the magisterial offices. In churches where there is a preponderance of the official element and its exclusive authority, there is possibly also an impoverishment of their spiritual power. The church may become a private club of the clergy. There is a need for an equilibrium of authority and power at every level in the church.

The ecumenical discussion of authority in the church should really be a three-sided dialog involving Catholics, mainline Protestants, and free-church traditions. The Eastern Orthodox are a special case, and may perform a valuable ecumenical service to the divided church in Western Christendom by showing how to strike a balance between the official, canonical, and charismatic dimensions of the one, holy, catholic, and apostolic church. However, there are some huge obstacles that stand in the way, such as their weak exilic presence in the West, their bondage to fierce ethnic loyalties, their esoteric mystical type of spirituality, the precritical naiveté of their theological methodology, and their lack of a vigorous missionary history and consciousness. Nevertheless, if our theological imagination is permitted to stretch far enough, we may discover beneath the layers of archaic forms an original synthesis of elements that have come apart in the West through schism after schism.

In any future synthesis of ministerial offices in the church, the Catholic line of development, including priesthood, episcopacy, and papacy, will retain its legitimacy. Transformations and reforms will continue under the impact of scriptural study and modern needs. As the notion of the Eucharist as sacrifice is revised in light of Scripture, the conception of the priesthood will also shift accordingly. No minister was called a priest in the New Testament church, because there was no sacrifice at which a priesthood would have to preside. Nor were those who presided at the Eucharist in the early church ever called priests. And the episcopal office will be bound to change as it sheds its one-sided legalistic Roman trappings in favor of a more collegial model of service. The papal office will continue to modernize itself in a direction 180° removed from what is implied in the dogma of infallibility.

Likewise, the history of Reformation Protestantism will bring its experience of the gospel nourished by its concentrated focus on the apostolic canon of Scripture. The *sola scriptura* principle expresses the norm by which the church norms all its doctrines, because the canon conveys the message of Christ. This principle has been surrendered by many self-professing Protestants, because they are unable to understand how the Scriptures can escape the fate of historical relativism. This loss of the scripture principle explains why modern theology has become a fashion parade of adjectival theologies— existentialist, process, scientific, liberation, feminist, etc. Nevertheless, the Scriptures will continue to mediate the apostolic substance of the faith to the contemporary church in spite of the ideological captivity of such modish theologies.

Free churches historically have their eye on the fact that there is free spiritual authority and power in the life of believers not exclusively tied to the Word and sacraments dispensed by ordained officials. The faith of the *laos* cannot be leashed to an official order, because the Word and Spirit are not locked up in the office to which only bishops hold the key. However, free-church history has experienced the danger on the other side, that when charismatic leaders take charge of a congregation, subject to no rules of canon law or book of discipline, they are frequently more despotic and authoritarian than any set of ecclesiastical officials. Charismatic power is difficult to check, because those who possess it claim to have been zapped directly by the Spirit.

In a comprehensive view of apostolic authority in the church today, it seems that all three roots are indispensable. Our churches need a creative interplay of official authority, canonical witness, and spiritual power, in new structures that combine checks and balances. John Naisbitt, author of *Megatrends: Ten New Directions Transforming Our Lives,* makes some useful observations. "Centralized structures are crumbling all across America."[11] The trend is from representative democracy to participatory democracy. And another: "For centuries, the pyramid structure was the way we organized and managed ourselves."[12] The trend is from hierarchies to networking. Networks are people talking to each other, sharing ideas, information, and resources. There should be an ecclesial model of this networking, because something like it was going on in the apostolic communities of early Christianity. Of course, the church has no duty to follow the current trends, no matter how mega, but it is free to use a combination of apostolic inspiration and secular wisdom to break away from rigidified patterns that merely reflect the megatrends of ancient, medieval, reformation, or modern times.

A worldwide ecumenical breakthrough on the doctrine of the ministry will take place when the *kairos* is ripe for holding a new universal council of all Christian churches that accept a joint invitation issued by the World Council of Churches and the Roman Catholic church. The ancient principle of conciliarity will need to be reestablished. In such a new series of ecumenical councils the greatest need will not be the accent of aggiornamento, as it was at Vatican II. Much of American Christianity has already modernized itself to the point of being out of touch with its apostolic roots. Each church tradition will need to bring its own strengths and be open to those of the others. The three lines we have been pursuing will need to be taken up in a creative synthesis: a theological retrieval of the apostolic message, a structural reformation of the apostolic ministry, and a generous welcome of charismatic renewal movements often working on the fringes of the organized churches.

8

The Ecumenical Problem
of Ordination and Succession

Luther's Dilemma on Ordination and Succession

In the previous chapter we located the problem of ministry in the history of the transmission of the authority of Christ and the gospel from apostolic to postapostolic times. The theological problem became: How can the apostolic church continue to be true to the apostolic witness after all the apostles have died? How could their authority be channeled through the coming generations? Our answer was: canon *and* office. The church of later times can remain close to Jesus Christ only through the office of preaching and teaching the apostolic Word and witness passed on through the canonical Scriptures. In this chapter we will focus more closely on the ecumenical problem of the appropriate office or offices to be entrusted with the authentic transmission of the apostolic voice of authority. We will begin with the peculiar way in which the problem strikes Lutheranism, which stands in a pivotal position between Catholics and Evangelicals on the doctrine of the ministry.

The Lutheran perplexity on the nature of the ministry can be traced to a basic inconsistency in Luther's thought.[1] This inconsistency continues to bedevil the Lutheran church in the 20th century. Neither

Luther's understanding of justification by faith nor his interpretation of Scripture provided him with an unambiguous position over against the Roman Catholic view of the ministry as a sacerdotal priesthood, or that of the Protestant enthusiasts who retained no special office of the ministry.

In his writing *On the Councils and the Church* Luther listed the office of the ministry as a fifth mark of the church, after the Word, Baptism, the Lord's Supper, and absolution. For the sake of the gospel it is necessary for the church to have the office of the ministry.

All Christians are members of the universal priesthood by virtue of Baptism. In principle, every Christian is endowed with the right to preach and administer the sacraments. Yet, the community calls and ordains someone to the public performance of these services. All Christians are priests, but not all are pastors.

What was Luther trying to say? Is the office of the ministry based on the priesthood of all Christians or did Christ himself institute it? Luther scholars and Lutheran theologians are divided on the answer to this question. Each side tends to force Luther into a mold of consistency, to agree with its own dogmatic preference. The one side holds that the ministry is a holy office based explicitly on a divine ordinance. God has commanded and instituted the office of the Word. The other side claims that, for Luther, all Christians are commissioned to be servants of the Word, but the rights of all are transferred to a few to avoid confusion. Are these two points of view like poles in a dialectical tension, or are we confronted with sheer contradiction? I share the hypothesis that Luther can justifiably be quoted on both sides. In his polemical writings from 1519 to 1523 Luther derived the office from the universal priesthood. Later Luther stressed more emphatically the divine institution of the office.

As a theologian, Luther was an occasionalist, not a systematician. He wrote on the run, meeting crisis after crisis. This is particularly evident in his writings on the church and the ministry. Lutheran churches around the world have participated in the ecumenical search for a theology of the ministry that might overcome the obstacles to reunion. They have not been able to discover in Luther firm foundations.[2] Rather, their recourse to Luther has more often confirmed whatever preferences they sought to vindicate. In pushing the demands of a radical laicism, Luther is remembered as the champion of the people against the priestly tyranny of Rome, and therefore against clerical monopoly of power. Those fighting this battle will quote Luther to desacralize ordination and discount its chain-like connection with a succession of officeholders. Was not the universal priesthood of believers the great religious principle of the Reformation, inviting each believer to intercede with God directly, apart from the mediatorial function of the priesthood? Does not this principle also entail the laity's right of private interpretation of the Bible, without bowing to the magisterial authority of popes and bishops? Luther in his "tower room" became for Protestant Christians the picture of the truly liberated man. Consequently, the church is pictured as primarily a group of individual believers who gather together to share their private experiences. Who then is the minister? The facilitator! The person with the skills to draw out the potential of each and build a group. The minister is the one who has been delegated by the group to perform certain functions in behalf of all. This doctrine is called the "transference theory," from the German *Übertragungslehre*. It makes the office a function of the congregation. Today it is called the "functionalist" view of the ministry. In rejecting the Roman doctrine of the priesthood, it levels down the church, quoting Luther, "All Christians are preachers, and all preachers are Christians"—statements that are false on both ends. The problem with this view is that it can make no clear distinction between the office of the ministry and the priesthood of all believers.

Many Lutherans feel confident they can appeal to Luther to support their functionalist view of the ministry. In speaking of the ministry of the Word, they start with the universal priesthood, and accordingly place a low value on ordination. The ministry is nothing more than the exercise of rights and privileges that originally belong to all, which they have delegated to one functionary for the sake of good order. The minister then becomes a mouthpiece of the congregation. This is a view that appeals to the democratic and congregationalist temperament of Americans. It has been taught by many Lutheran dogmaticians and church leaders, and now has a

fairly strong grip on the minds of those who manage the bureau-
cracies of the church. Luther speculated about what would have to
happen in an emergency situation, if a group of lay folk should find
themselves on a desert island without a preacher. They could choose
any one of them to preach, administer the sacraments, and, in general, exercise the office of the keys. Ordination in that emergency
situation would mean nothing. Ironically, congregational Lutherans
have developed a doctrine of the ministry on the model of an emergency situation, but in practice they have incongruously retained the
rite of ordination. As ordination is taking place, they mutter to
themselves, "It is not a sacrament; it bestows no *character inde-
lebilis*; this is not a *sign* of succession leading back to the apostles."
It is just a ceremony, but they do not know what they are doing, or
what for.

We can readily see how this idea of the minister's status determines the question of authority. In our democratic system of thinking, when people no longer feel they are being fairly represented
by their delegated representative, they can terminate the contract.
They pay the minister's salary, after all. If they are not getting their
money's worth, they can trade their minister in for another. It takes
no great imagination to see that the psychological and sociological
ramifications of the minister's dilemma actually have deep roots in
a doctrinal question. This route leads to a tremendous loss of apostolic substance. It opens the way for Christianity to become a civil
religion at the mercy of popular trends and the electronic media.

Contemporary Luther-scholarship has robbed the "transference
theory" of the right to claim his solid support. The more widely
supported view is that Luther shifted his emphasis in later years,
when he found that his more conservative reformation was being
outflanked by the radical reformers. He then put greater stress on
the importance of the office. There is no reason to rob from Peter
to pay Paul, to play the office of the ministry off against the charism
of the Spirit granted to every believer in Baptism. Both the preaching
office and the general priesthood are founded by divine institution,
and this divine institution is ultimately based on the work of Christ.
The "transference theory" depends on a highly selective use of

Luther's statements fired off in the heat of battle against the presumptuous claims of the Roman hierarchy.

Opposed to the "transference theory" is that of the divine institution of the office through Christ himself and the apostles, and not first through the Spirit-filled members of the congregation. American Lutherans have inherited the tensions and contradictions in Luther's understanding of the ministry from the 19th-century controversies surrounding the views of C. F. W. Walther and Wilhelm Löhe. Lutherans in North America were involved in bitter disputes concerning the nature of the church and its ministry.[3] The dispute began between J. A. A. Grabau of the Buffalo Synod and C. F. W. Walther of the Missouri Synod over practical church matters: the excommunication of pastors and congregations by one party and their acceptance by the other. It is instructive to be reminded of this almost forgotten chapter in American Lutheran church history, because the issues raised at that time have come back to haunt us in the process of creating a new Lutheran church body in the U.S.A.

On the one side was Grabau's episcopal view of the nature of the church and its ministry, and on the other was Walther's congregationalism, which the Missouri Synod accepted at its founding in 1846. Grabau wrote a pastoral letter to his congregations in 1840, outlining his view of the ministry, and sent a copy to the Missouri Saxons. He dealt with the question whether a group of Christians without a pastor can take it upon themselves to ordain a person out of their midst to administer the sacraments and perform other pastoral duties. Grabau's answer was an emphatic "No." That person would not have a valid call. Any pastor without a valid call is not entitled to exercise the duties of the office, give absolution, or administer the Lord's Supper. That person would be distributing nothing more than mere bread and wine. A congregation may only call a pastor whom the Synod ordains, and the Synod is made up exclusively of the ministerium. It is clear that the Synod of pastors comes before the congregation, and that ordination is mediated aristocratically through the ministerium and not democratically through the congregation.

Walther saw in Grabau's view the kind of autocratic tyranny the Saxons had suffered at the hands of their deposed founder and leader,

Martin Stephan. He agreed that the preaching office was a divine institution, but held that it grew out of the priesthood of all believers. The congregation possesses the authority of the office but, for the sake of good order, transfers it to one of its members. Wilhelm Löhe had friends on both sides of the dispute and tried to reconcile the two opposing factions. But his theological sympathies lay on the side of Grabau, as he preferred a high view of the ministerial office, believing that it goes back to the apostles. All Christians are ministers to those *outside* the church; the ordained have the authority of preaching and teaching *within* the church. The office was established by Christ and the apostles and does not come from the community. For Walther ordination is a human ceremony, a kind of *adiaphoron*. For Löhe, ordination confers a spiritual charism upon the individual.

Such is the Lutheran legacy on the church and its ministry. Lutherans have lived with these tensions and contradictions. The last decades have witnessed one comprehensive study after the other on the doctrine of the ministry in all the Lutheran church bodies, and each one of them has tried to walk a tightrope between two views on the ministry that can be traced back to Luther's own teachings. This lack of decisiveness has placed the ministry on shaky foundations and threatens the primacy of the means of grace in the divine administration of the church. If the transference theory is correct, the minister has no real authority, and, worse than that, what authority the minister does have is taken from the laity. The lack of a clear view of the ministerial office reflects itself in a great deal of confusion about the relation of the laity to the ministry. The trend to laicize the clergy is correlative to the trend to clericalize the laity. The way to recover the lay apostolate is not merely by making lay people more active in the church and more visible in liturgical roles, but by helping the laity to be the diaspora church in the world.

At the Ecumenical Crossroads

The ministry has become the most debated topic on the ecumenical agenda. To clarify the problems of the ministry in present-day Christianity we are going to take up certain ecumenically significant discussions, leading up to the Faith and Order statement (sometimes called the Lima text, named from the place of its adoption) entitled *Baptism, Eucharist and Ministry.*

Roman Catholic theology, on the basis of biblical studies, has developed a new understanding of the church as "people of God" and of the ministry as *diakonia.* This has helped it to bring about considerable rapprochement with traditions that stem from the Reformation. Luther's emphasis on the universal priesthood of believers has been reclaimed as an essential part of the Catholic tradition. Roman Catholic theology can now say: Now that we are taking seriously the universal priesthood and are responding to Luther's appeal for a full integration of all Christians into the fullness of the church, what are you Protestants doing to attain a fuller realization of the manifold structures of the church? Hans Küng has put some questions from a Catholic perspective with which all churches must grapple, the answers to which are gradually being developed as churches find themselves moving on converging paths in the direction of the Lima definitions of ministry.

Küng asks, "Is ecclesiastical office necessary for theological or sociological reasons? Does the institution of ecclesiastical office originate with Christ or the church? Is the episcopal office required in the church or not? Is the episcopal office based on divine or human law? Does it include bishops in the strict sense of the word or does it merely refer to pastors? Is the desire for a Protestant episcopal office an expression of the Reformation or of political expediency? Is ecclesiastical office elective or appointive? Is the ordination of office an official legitimation (a confirmation of the vocation) or is it a 'consecration' (an essential factor of the vocation itself)? Is ordination required by divine law or human law? Are the 'rites' of ordination to be understood as church ceremony or as Sacrament of the church? Is the officeholder an agent of God or of the congregation?"[4] These are the kinds of questions Lutherans meet at the ecumenical crossroads. They can no longer pretend to be able to answer them satisfactorily out of Luther's theology or the *Book of Concord.*

However far Lutherans find it possible to move toward a new ecumenical consensus on the ministry, they will surely wish to bring along the strength of their distinctive confessional emphases. We have previously argued that there are two channels of apostolic succession, canon and office. If Lutherans have been weak on office, they have been strong on canon. They should not now allow the pendulum to swing to the other side, along with the episcopal traditions, which have been strong on office and weak on canon. Luther and the confessional writings are correct in emphasizing the priority of the Word of God and its authority over popes, bishops, councils, and synods. They are also correct in interpreting apostolic succession as a succession in the apostolic spirit, faith, and confession. But is that all? Can this view satisfactorily counter the charge of ecclesiological docetism? Granted that the Word of God is the authority in the church, what are the appropriate mediating structures of that authority? Does it work invisibly by osmosis? That fits the view of the church as made up of true believers who belong to the invisible church. But what is the channel of apostolic authority in the visible church, which is the only one which needs theology after all? This docetism goes along with a certain Lutheran tendency to "enthusiasm" (*Schwärmerei*), in the sense Luther applied to the left-wing radicals. But Luther's own teaching on ministry is tainted by a certain spiritualizing of the office. Grabau called the Missouri ministers who started up their own ministry from the laity "*Rottenprediger.*" Their ordination was not valid. The transference theory is false doctrine, even if it can boast of some choice quotations of Luther.

All Christians have the right to interpret the Scriptures; all are subject to the authority of the Word of God. Does this principle of lay universality mean that no further distinctions need to be made? It is at this point that the Catholic tradition challenges Protestants. The authority of a pastor is not the same as that of a congregational meeting. The office does not exist merely for the sake of good order, but as a channel of apostolic authority. Ordination is not merely the transfer of the rights of the many to a single person. The office is not based on a human arrangement (*ius humanum*) but on divine institution (*ius divinum*). Ordination, therefore, has some kind of sacramental significance, as Melanchthon himself allowed: "If ordination is interpreted in relation to the ministry of the Word, we have no objection to calling ordination a sacrament. . . . If ordination is interpreted this way, we shall not object either to calling the laying on of hands a sacrament.''[5] Well, if there is really no objection, let us call ordination a sacrament, for, as Melanchthon continues, ''we know that God approves this ministry and is present in it. It is good to extol the ministry of the Word with every possible kind of praise in opposition to the fanatics who dream that the Holy Spirit does not come through the Word.''[6]

It has been salutary for Lutherans to feel the pressure of the Catholic partners in the ecumenical dialogs. The Catholic-Lutheran dialog in the United States published its findings on the ministry in *Eucharist and Ministry* (1970). Here we find the Lutheran participants in the vanguard of a healthy trend toward the recovery of a theology of a special ministry in the church. Their common statement defined the special ministry as ''a specific order, function, or gift (charism) within and for the sake of Christ's church in its mission to the world.''[7] They agreed that the office is not identical with nor derived from the universal priesthood. The transference theory is rejected. ''God instituted the sacred Ministry of teaching the gospel and administering the sacraments.''[8] This ministry has the task of proclaiming the gospel to the world and of building up the community. Through Word and sacraments the special ministry serves to unify and order the church for its mission to the world. The Catholic participants were pleased to hear their Lutheran partners stress Article 14 of the Augsburg Confession: ''we say that no one should be allowed to administer the word and the sacraments in the church unless he is duly called.'' The words for ''duly called'' are *rite vocatus* in Latin, and in this context they mean, purely and simply, ordination. These Lutherans agreed that ordination is no *adiaphoron,* but that it ultimately comes from Christ and confers a spiritual authority on the recipient in a once-for-all fashion.

So close did these theologians come to a consensus that the Catholic theologians could make the statement: ''We see no persuasive reason to deny the possibility of the Roman Catholic church recognizing the validity of this Ministry. Accordingly we ask the authorities of the Roman Catholic church whether the ecumenical urgency flowing from Christ's will for unity may not dictate that the Roman Catholic church recognize the validity of the Lutheran

Ministry and, correspondingly, the presence of the body and blood of Christ in the eucharistic celebrations of the Lutheran churches.''[9]

This dialog left open the question of how to order the special ministry. Catholics hold to the classical threefold order: deacon, priest (presbyter), and bishop. Lutherans have only one order of ordained ministers. How serious a defect is the lack of episcopal ordination and succession on the part of Lutherans? Is presbyteral succession sufficient to secure continuity with the apostolic ministry? The original Lutherans had no intention of getting rid of the traditional episcopal order and discipline of the church. They were simply stuck with the undesirable fact that no bishop was willing to ordain pastors for evangelical congregations. In this dialog, Lutherans admitted that they are in principle free to take steps to recover an episcopal structure and polity.

The issue of episcopal ordination and succession has become more acute for Lutherans in their encounter with the Anglican tradition. A prime testing ground in unifying the ministries of episcopal and nonepiscopal churches is offered by the Church of South India. One of the major problems in consummating this union was the problem of the ministry. Their success will make it a likely model of similar efforts around the world. Three main options faced the church bodies in the union negotiations: (1) adoption of a nonepiscopal form of ministry; (2) adoption of not only the structure of the historic episcopacy, but also its Anglo-Catholic interpretation, making episcopacy a *conditio sine qua non;* (3) espousing the historic episcopacy, apart from any theory about its nature and necessity. The third course was followed. Details of practice were worked out so that the church would be equipped with bishops whose succession was indisputable. From the time of union all ministers are episcopally ordained. In these doctrinal negotiations, Lutherans made no objection to the fact of episcopacy, but they refused to accept it as essential to the doctrine of the gospel by which the church stands or falls. It may be agreed that episcopal order is a valid and valuable form of the church, but Lutherans could not unite with a church which confuses episcopal order with evangelical faith.[10] Ordination by episcopal laying on of hands does not necessarily make a church apostolic in its faith and doctrine. Nevertheless, it may certainly be a form of ministry instituted for that purpose. It may fail, and so may every other form of ministry. *Abusum non tollit usum*!

Edmund Schlink has offered Lutherans a formulation that can prove helpful in dialog with Anglicans or Episcopalians. "It [i.e., succession through ordination by episcopal laying on of hands] is not the *sine qua non* of the apostolic succession of church and ministry. It does not produce an apostolic succession and authority which are missing from the other types of ordination. Already during the christological conflicts of the patristic church, it did not prove to be the unfailing remedy securing the apostolicity of church and dogma, and this became clear as church history unfolded itself. On the other hand, we must see in the episcopal laying on of hands a *sign* for the apostolic succession of the ministries and the church. It is a sign which is used to demonstrate that the church is Christ's church only when it is conscious of being founded on the apostles. The succession of episcopal laying on of hands is therefore a sign for the unity and catholicity of the church. . . . We should therefore welcome the successive laying on of hands by bishops all through church history as a *sign* of apostolicity, and if it is absent, it is right for us to work for its introduction."[11] That seems to me to be a theologically and practically sane view of the matter of episcopal ordination and succession.

It has become all the easier for Lutherans to enter into altar and pulpit fellowship with The Episcopal Church because the High Church Anglican theology of episcopal ministry has been losing ground. A fairly standard view among Anglicans was presented by a group of Anglican theologians on the occasion of the Church of South India union, in a book entitled *The Historic Episcopacy*. This book succeeded in transcending the old debate on episcopacy as belonging either to the *esse* (being) or merely the *bene esse* (well-being) of the church's ministry. In their place it proposed the formula *plene esse* (fullness of being). In his chapter, Bishop John A. T. Robinson described the historic episcopate as "the outward and visible expression at once of the church's catholicity and of its apostolicity. . . . Every scheme for Christian unity must come to terms with the historic episcopate; for despite it the church cannot in fact be fully one, catholic or apostolic.[12] Even if we can find no doctrinal reasons deeply embedded in the gospel, there are sufficient reasons from tradition to view the historic episcopacy as a part of the *plene esse* of the church. At least Lutherans should be prepared to say that they will cheerfully accept the historic episcopacy on the condition that as a ministry within the whole church, it really functions to transmit the historic faith to every new generation and to serve as a sign of living continuity with the apostolic ministry.

On a totally different front the quest for a solution to the ecumenical problem of the ministry is being pursued. The Church of Christ Uniting (COCU) is a movement among ten American Protestant denominations to discover new patterns of unity in eucharistic fellowship and the mutual recognition of ministries. COCU dates back to what historians call the Blake-Pike proposal. On December 4, 1960, Dr. Eugene Carson Blake preached a sermon in Grace Cathedral in San Francisco entitled "A Proposal Toward the Reunion of Christ's Church." He summoned Presbyterians, Episcopalians, Methodists, and the United Church of Christ to form a plan of union that would be both catholic and reformed. Later, other denominations joined the movement—the Disciples and the Brethren, among others. Not surprisingly, the doctrine of the ministry has become the chief hurdle in uniting episcopal, presbyterial, and congregational systems.

Lutherans have not become a part of COCU. Lutherans would have a lot to gain and something to contribute to COCU, but generally they feel more at ease dialoging about theological issues that divide them from Roman Catholics than discussing matters of church order with American Protestants. A Lutheran gets the impression that, among these Protestants, all other important doctrinal issues are settled. What they really care about is church order. They would all seem to agree with Karl Barth: "Church order has to do with the nature of the Church."[13] But they have not been able to agree on what kind.

The COCU plan of union has reaped the benefits of prior attempts to merge presbyterial and episcopal polities. In 1957 a report entitled "Relations between Anglican and Presbyterian Churches" was published simultaneously in London and Edinburgh. The proposal called for a modification of church polities which would give bishops to Presbyterians and elders to Anglicans. The working formula was "bishops-in-presbytery." Oversight in the church—*episcopē* means "oversight"—would rest in a bishop-in-presbytery. The bishop chosen by the particular presbytery would be consecrated by bishops from existing Episcopal churches, and would be the principal minister in every ordination from then on. Many Presbyterians have not been able to swallow the inescapable implication that ministers of Presbyterian churches now have a somewhat deficient status, a deficiency that can be remedied only by returning to the historical chain of episcopal succession through ordination.

Whereas the ecumenical pressure is intense for Protestants to take the historic episcopate seriously, their secular democratic context in the United States pulls them in the opposite direction. In 1961 the United Presbyterian Church in the U.S.A. published an impressive study on the ministry, claiming that it is not *proper orders* but *proper functions* that count in the ministry. There is, throughout, a gospel-centered and service-directed understanding of the ministry. Ministry is simply serving the world with the gospel of Christ. Every Christian must participate in the total ministry of the church: worship, vocation, and order. The ministry of order is for the sake of special ministries doing Christ's mission in the world. There is a surprising freedom in this document from any sense of having to preserve a specifically presbyteral type of order, let alone an episcopal one. It recognizes no single pattern in the New Testament, no such thing as one kind of primitive church order. "This means—and it is often a hard lesson for Presbyterians, among others, to learn—that every effort in subsequent centuries to use the Bible as a book of canon law, or manual of polity, inevitably lapses either into frustration or into nonsense."[14] It continues: "The blunt fact is that we are given no supernatural polity in the New Testament."[15] This study concludes that the special ministry is essential, indeed, but no particular way of structuring the church's ministry is essential or necessarily permanent. The test to apply with respect to any structure is: Will it aid or impede the mission of the church? This study was even willing to use this missiological criterion in relation to ordination by laying on of hands, not to mention the office of the bishop. The church which is reformed and is always being reformed (*ecclesia reformata sed semper reformanda*) must beware lest any of its forms or offices foster superstition or remain too inflexible for mission in a changing world.

The Presbyterians in this study adopted a strictly functionalist view of the ministry. It fits the mind-set of American pragmatism. The meaning of ministerial ordination was downplayed in favor of the idea that Baptism alone offers the real ordination into the royal priesthood. The ordination of ministers does not mean anything else than appointment to special tasks. "But such ordination in no sense creates a separate, or separated, order or class. There can be divisions of function within the body but no distinctions of 'status.' "[16] The upshot of this view is what the Presbyterian committee on the ministry called "the instrumental view of the Christian ministry."[17] This view is to the Presbyterians what the "transference theory" of the ministry is to the Lutherans.

The irony is that, at precisely the same time that the Presbyterians were descending to a pragmatic view of the ministry, accommodating the American Zeitgeist, they were being called into a plan of union with Episcopalians who had no intention of loosening their links with the doctrine and practice of episcopal ordination and succession.[18]

Can COCU succeed? The answer to this question coincides with the question whether the Faith and Order Lima statement on the ministry will be widely received throughout world Christianity. The problems are precisely the same.[19] What is the relationship between the ordained ministry and the ministry of all the baptized? What is apostolic and how is this apostolicity maintained and passed on from one generation to another? Can the idea of episcopal succession be accepted by nonepiscopal traditions as an effective *sign* of the continuity of the church in apostolic faith and mission, although not an automatic guarantee? Can the episcopal traditions accept the idea that the succession of apostolic faith has been maintained in churches without an episcopal pipeline to the apostles, which in any case is only an *ex post facto* theory without historical backing? Can the churches together devise an office of apostolic *episcopē* in a reunited church of the future? All churches are being confronted with these challenging questions. All churches claim to possess a kind of apostolic succession. They all regard their ministries as mediating continuity with the apostles. The difference is that American Lutheran pastors lack the sign of transmission through ordination by a bishop who was ordained by a bishop. Why not adopt this sign? What stands in the way? It would provide all our churches with a common symbol of unity, expressing continuity with the ministry of the apostles.

COCU may point the way for Lutherans. Lutheran bishops are now primarily administrative officers, not bishops in either the New Testament or the traditional sense. The COCU document on ministry describes the ministry of bishops as personal, collegial, and constitutional. Their responsibility is described in the following terms: liturgical leader, teacher of apostolic faith, pastoral overseer, leader in mission, representative minister of ordination, administrative leader, and servant of unity. There is much to commend this proposal. The church has always had this kind of ministry from very early days. To be sure, the ministry of bishops has been horribly distorted in church history, but on the whole and in the long run, it has served the church well in the past and continues to do so today among three-fourths of the world's Christians.

There is a great worry that the return of the episcopal form of ministry will lead to the abuse of power and cripple lay initiatives. People remember the autocratic and aristocratic roles bishops played in imperial times. In the American context, bishops will never be granted such arbitrary power. A clear distinction must be made between power and authority. Bishops may have authority, but their power will necessarily be limited by democratic arrangements involving the laity at local, regional, national, and international levels. People are asking that their bishops return more to the apostolic model, and become less oriented to management and administration and more intentionally pastoral and sacramental. Churches in COCU have the opportunity to recover some of the classical virtues of the historic episcopate, while eschewing the autocratic abuses of prelacy.

The theme of "ministry and order" has been on the agenda of Faith and Order of the World Council of Churches since the Edinburgh conference in 1937 and was again at the Montreal conference in 1963. At Montreal there were a few clearly formulated points on which delegates could agree.[20] Here the foundations were laid on which the Lima statement on ministry could build. A pattern was created which is universally reflected in the statements on ministry of individual church commissions. It begins with a recognition of the royal priesthood of the whole people of God, making ministry a responsibility of the whole body of baptized believers. This ministry in turn is placed within the context of the totality of human existence in the world of which Christ is professed as Lord. Within the universal ministry of all believers, there is a special ministry. There is no agreement on what to call this special ministry in distinction from the ministry of the whole church. There is no agreement on the relationship and distinction between them, or on what is and what is not included in the special ministry. The whole church and its special ministry have their origin in Christ's sending of the apostles. The mission of the apostles is continued by the church and its ministry. Jesus Christ has given ministers to his church, to build it up and to equip it. Ministers are servants of the servants of God. Ministers preach the Word, administer the sacraments, watch in prayer, lead God's people, and engage in deeds of Christian love. But in some way the whole church shares in this stewardship. The Holy Spirit gives a variety of gifts; the special ministry is one among them. The Holy Spirit may call persons into the special ministry through the community or individually, but in every case the exercise of the special ministers requires the acknowledgment and confirmation of the church. This confirmation is given in ordination, consisting in prayer and the laying on of hands. The statement then notes: "The orderly transmission of authority in ordination is normally an essential part of the means by which the Church is kept from generation to generation in the apostolic faith."[21] All churches regard such continuity in the apostolic faith as essential. Some of them believe the unbroken succession of episcopal ordination from the apostles is a necessary guarantee of a valid ministry and of the

safeguarding of the true faith, and that such ordination is a sacrament. Other churches would rather emphasize that the Spirit can
and does create new forms of order, is not bound to one, and that
the New Testament does not clearly warrant setting persons apart
through ordination for a lifetime of ministry in the church.

Montreal provided a basic inventory of the agreements and differences between the churches. That is now over 20 years ago. In
the meantime, so much progress was made that at Lima, Peru, in
1982, over 100 delegates from the same churches, including Roman
Catholic representatives, unanimously adopted the statement entitled
Baptism, Eucharist and Ministry. The history of this statement cov-
ers a 50-year process; it went through numerous stages of development which need not concern us here. What is of momentous
significance is its *kairotic* character. The time is ripe for the churches
to seize the moment of opportunity and capitalize on an ecumenical
breakthrough that might serve as the next step toward the convocation of a universal council of churches at which the ministries of
our divided churches might be mutually recognized.

At the time of this writing, all churches are busy preparing an
official response to the Lima text. They are asked whether they can
recognize in it the faith of the church through the ages. If Lutherans
find it possible to participate positively in the ongoing process of
reception, and we anticipate they will, they will have moved a long
way toward the resolution of the dilemma which they inherited from
the schism at the Reformation. No one is claiming that this document
expresses a full consensus among the churches, only that its agreement is sufficient to embolden churches to take further steps together
toward the goal of visible unity.

Now to some of the most important items in this text. The text
begins with some central affirmations of the catholic faith under the
rubric ''The Calling of the Whole People of God.'' In six paragraphs
the whole story of salvation is recited. Here we have basic Christological, trinitarian, eschatological, and missiological confessions
on which it is hoped the churches can agree. Under the rubric of
''The Church and the Ordained Ministry'' a high view of the special
ministry is set forth. Will all churches really be able to join in the
consensus? Will all Lutherans agree with the following position

statements? (1) The ordained ministry is constitutive for the life and witness of the church. (2) Ministers are needed to point to the church's fundamental dependence on Jesus Christ and to provide a focus of unity within a multiplicity of gifts. (3) The church has always had persons holding specific authority and responsibility, beginning with the Twelve and then the apostles. That process of calling and sending is continuing through the action of Christ and the Holy Spirit. (4) Ordained ministers are called heralds, ambassadors, leaders, teachers, and pastors, representing Jesus Christ, his message and authority to the community. (5) The authority of the ordained ministry is rooted in Jesus Christ and is modeled on his unique life of service, not on autocratic domination. (6) Although it is recognized that the New Testament does not mandate a single pattern of ministry, and that the church in its history has structured its ministry in different ways, yet—and here is the challenge—"the threefold ministry of bishop, presbyter and deacon may serve today as an expression of the unity we seek and also as a means for achieving it. Historically, it is true to say, the threefold ministry became the generally accepted pattern in the church of the early centuries and is still retained today by many churches. In the fulfillment of their mission and service the churches need people who in different ways express and perform the tasks of the ordained ministry in its diaconal, presbyterial and episcopal aspects and functions." (7) The ministry of *episcopē* is a necessary one to express and safeguard the unity of the church.

The Lima text acknowledges that churches which have retained the threefold ministry will need to reform it in order to release its potential for the mission of the church in the world. And churches which do not possess it should ask themselves whether the threefold ministry does not have a powerful claim to be accepted by them. But the proposal is not rigid. There is leeway as to how churches should define the functions of bishops, presbyters (pastors), and deacons. Nor is there anything sacrosanct about the titles as such. But some tentative definitions are provided.

Bishops preach the Word and preside at the sacraments. They administer discipline as ministers of oversight, continuity, and unity in the church. They serve the apostolicity of the church and bear responsibility for leadership in the church's mission. They relate their community to the worldwide community and are responsible for the orderly transfer of ministerial authority in the church, namely, ordination. This is a far cry from the role of bishops in American Lutheranism, who function more like branch managers of a business corporation.

Presbyters are ministers of Word and sacraments in a local community. They do pretty much what a pastor is expected to do in a typical congregation—preach, teach, provide pastoral care, equip the laity for their ministries in the world, etc.

Deacons are servants of the church in the world, struggling to meet the needs of persons and societies. Theirs is a ministry of love. But that is not all. They also assist pastors in leading worship, reading the Scriptures, preaching, teaching, and leading in prayer. They may also assist in administration, evangelism, and stewardship. Since the diaconate has fallen on hard times in many churches, and since there is so much uncertainty about its status and its relation to the ordained ministry, we shall devote a special section to it.

On the issue of apostolic succession, it is affirmed that there is a succession of the apostolic tradition in the church as a whole. The ordained ministry has the task of preserving and actualizing the apostolic faith. The episcopal ministry is a sign, though not a guarantee, of the continuity and unity of the church. Will churches that have not enjoyed episcopal succession be willing to accept it as a *sign,* as Schlink proposed in behalf of Lutherans, of the apostolicity of the church as a whole? This does not mean that their own ministries are invalid until the time they are linked up with episcopal succession. The distinction between the *esse, bene esse,* and *plene esse,* which we already defined, can be useful at this point.

On the issue of ordination, this document carries us far beyond a mere church ceremony. It possesses a certain kind of sacramental validity, since we are told that "ordination denotes an action by God and the community by which the ordained are strengthened by the Spirit for their task."[22] "The act of ordination by the laying on of hands of those appointed to do so is at one and the same time invocation of the Holy Spirit (*epiclesis*); sacramental sign; acknowledgement of gifts and commitment."[23] Other similar words denoting

sacramental significance are used: "Ordination is a sign of the grant-
ing of this prayer by the Lord who gives the gift of the ordained
ministry. . . . The church ordains in confidence that God, being
faithful to his promise in Christ, enters sacramentally into contingent, historical forms of human relationship and uses them for his
purpose. Ordination is a sign performed in faith that the spiritual
relationship signified is present in, with and through the words spoken, the gestures made and the forms employed."[24] These words
suggest an analogy with the other sacramental actions of the church.
Just as some left-wing Protestants question whether Baptism and the
Eucharist are sacraments bestowing grace, so also there are many
mainstream Protestants, including Lutherans, who have denied to
ordination any sacramental aspect. The invocation and manumission
are mere ceremonial actions of the church, perhaps even very ancient
and meaningful ones, but fundamentally lacking any special pro-
ferring of a charism of the Spirit for ministry in Christ's church.

The question remains open at this time. Will our nonepiscopal
churches be willing to recover the sign of the episcopal succession
as a way of strengthening and deepening their continuity with the
apostolic witness and mission? The reason to do so is not merely
to please our episcopal friends or to advance the ecumenical movement and its quest for unity. The reason to do so is to promote the
mission of the church in the world. The New Testament word for
"order" is *tasso,* a military term. It was a word used for ordering
a fighting unit from a marching to a battle formation. The main
justification for reordering the ministry today—say, from the single
order of ordained pastors to the threefold order of bishops, pastors,
and deacons—is to marshal the forces of the church, especially at
the leadership level, to move out on its mission and expand its
campaign of service in the world. One congregation cannot take on
the regional, national, or global situation by itself. The church must
deploy itself for a broad course of action. The historic tradition of
the church argues in favor of the threefold ordering of ministry. It
has proven its usefulness in helping the church to deploy its forces
in carrying out the apostolic mission for the world.

The Ordination of Deacons

There are many committed persons who come to the seminary to study theology and prepare for ministry. Because they feel called and their synod or district endorses them they seek ordination. At the present time we have only one ordination, one place to deploy them, and that is into the pastoral office as leader of a local congregation. This happens in spite of the fact that many of these candidates obviously do not have the gifts of leadership. How shall they be placed in charge of a Christian community? They cannot preach and they cannot teach and they cannot lead in a way that equips the laity for their ministries in the world. Yet, they are called to service and they are able to serve in a multitude of ways. They should be deacons. "And the twelve summoned the body of the disciples and said, 'It is not right that we should give up preaching the word of God to serve tables. Therefore, brethren, pick out from among you seven men of good repute, full of the Spirit and of wisdom, whom we may appoint to this duty. But we will devote ourselves to prayer and to the ministry of the word.' And what they said pleased the whole multitude, and they chose Stephen, a man full of faith and of the Holy Spirit, and Philip. . . . These they set before the apostles, and they prayed and laid their hands upon them" (Acts 6:2-6). This is the earliest precedent of diaconal ordination. It was needed then, and it is even more needed now. We should recover the diaconal office as a life-long ministry commissioned by the church.

In order to motivate this call for the restoration of the diaconate, we must deal with its biblical roots as well as its wavering history in the church.

Diakonia had a number of meanings in common Greek usage. It meant waiting on tables, taking care of life's needs, or serving in any capacity whatever. In the eyes of Greek society, the role of the servant was regarded as inferior, debasing, and unworthy of a truly free and educated person. The aim of life was to become a master, to be served rather than to serve. The Sophist in one of Plato's dialogs says: "How could a man be happy, if he has to be a servant?"

This low view of the servant's status is bound up with Greek anthropology. The Greek sees the goal of life as the full development of the individual personality. Nowhere do we find the idea that one fulfills oneself by giving oneself in behalf of another.

Jesus' concept of service is rooted in the Old Testament commandment to love the neighbor. The basic attitude of a disciple of Jesus must be such love as is glad to serve. The new thing that Jesus brings about is a reversal in the customary relationship. Who is ordinarily thought to be the greater? Ordinarily, the one who sits at the table and is waited on. But Jesus changes this through his own life of service. Being a true servant puts one in a relationship that may entail sacrifice and suffering. The New Testament concept of ministry attains its ultimate sociological depth in the suffering servanthood of Jesus himself. His reversal of the normal human concepts of greatness and rank was dramatically acted out in his own life. "The Son of man did not come to be served but to serve, and to surrender his life as a ransom for many" (Mark 10:45).

The New Testament concept of *diakonia* makes clear that the purpose of human existence is the exact opposite of the pagan humanistic ideal of "successful living." The gifts which God gives are not to be cultivated to bring credit to our names, families, or nation. The purpose is service and that alone. "As each has received a gift, employ it for one another, as good stewards of God's varied grace: whoever speaks, as one who utters oracles of God; whoever renders service, as one who renders it by the strength which God supplies; in order that in everything God may be glorified through Jesus Christ. To him belong glory and dominion for ever and ever. Amen" (1 Peter 4:10-11).

This term *diakonia* has enormous significance for the doctrine of the church as a whole. The church is essentially the medium of Christ's kind of ministry. The church is composed of a variety of individuals and they have a variety of gifts to do a variety of good things. Charism and service go together. No one should be asked to perform a service for which there is no corresponding gift. If one does not have the gift to preach or teach, one should not be appointed to do these things. On the other hand, there are persons who can preach, teach, preside, and console, and should perhaps leave it to others to raise money, feed the poor, care for the sick, organize for advocacy, administer stewardship programs, and do a myriad of other things that the situation might demand.

Already in the New Testament there is a shift of meaning in the concept of *diakonia* from a purely functional sense to a special office. The office of the deacon became a distinct one alongside that of the bishop. In Phil. 1:1 Paul and Timothy greet the saints in Philippi, including their "bishops and deacons." Already by this time the office of the deacon was quite fully developed, and the deacon was the bishop's helper. To be sure, all Christians are called to be servants of Christ and of their neighbors, but still certain ones are selected to be deacons. The special functions of this office are quite clear in this early period.

Deacons were charged with looking after the department of stewardship and charity. They worked in close conjunction with bishops and carried out not only menial tasks but also instruction and consolation of those in need. Stephen and Philip, both deacons, also labored as evangelists. The church expressed its freedom to develop its ministries according to needs that arose, even when there was no express command from the Lord.

After the apostolic age the office of the deacon became a standard part of the governing body of the local church. Besides deacons there were bishops and presbyters. The bishops were regarded as successors of the apostles. The presbyters became the priests in the Catholic church, clothed with sacerdotal power. The deacons became subject to the priests. These three offices constituted the three clerical orders in distinction from the laity.

For the first several centuries the deacons preserved the basic functions of the apostolic period. They were in charge of the charitable funds of the congregation, they visited the aged, the widows, the sick and afflicted, the martyrs in prison, and they administered relief under the direction of the bishop. However, in the course of time this primary function became secondary and sometimes disappeared altogether, as the sick and the poor were gathered into hospitals and poorhouses, and the orphans into orphanages, and as each of these institutions came to be administered by its own staff. What then happened was that deacons became the assistants in public worship, especially at Baptism and Holy Communion. They arranged the altar, took up the offerings, read the lessons, recited prayers, and occasionally preached. They were also the deputies and advisors of the bishops. It is clear that this office became thoroughly ecclesiasticized; deacons became preoccupied with religious activities. No longer were they the church's arms of mercy in the world. The diaconate had become a stage on the way to the priesthood, rather than a station of service from which the church reached out into the world.

In Protestantism the diaconate has not always fared so well either. In the Anglican church the diaconate became merely a point of transition to the priesthood. In the Lutheran church the term *diaconus* was a title used of assistant pastors or chaplains of subordinate rank. Luther himself desired the restoration of the apostolic deacons for the care of the poor and the property of the church. The Reformed churches, with their zeal for recovering the primitive structure of the New Testament church, did more to revive the diaconate. Calvin regarded the diaconate as one of the indispensable offices of the church, and the care of the poor as the proper duty of deacons.

In the 19th century a new development in the concept of the diaconate took place in Germany. In 1833 Johann Hinrich Wichern established the Raues Haus near Hamburg as a rescue home for neglected children. Industrialization was bringing in its wake an increasing number of victims of the emerging social order. There developed a need for highly trained persons who would be able to meet the needs of orphans and destitute children, the sick, feeble-minded and insane people, epileptics, alcoholics, prisoners, etc. So Wichern established a community to train young men to take up various kinds of work in institutions. The candidates came mostly from the humbler classes, with simple Christian piety, devotion, and charity. Wichern's work became a model for the extension of the inner mission work in Germany. To begin with, the members of this movement were called "brothers," but soon they called themselves "deacons." At about the same time, a pastor by the name of Theodor Fliedner started work among women, and from this movement there developed the deaconess homes which still survive but are hardly flourishing.

If today the diaconal dimension of the church's life in Christ is to be revived, the concept of *diakonia* must be kept in the closest possible connection with at least two other dimensions of ministry. They are the liturgical (*leitourgia*) and the witnessing (*martyria*) dimensions. In *leitourgia* the community of Christ receives with prayer and praise the presence of its Lord, and in *martyria* the community proclaims the coming reign of God in the name of Jesus. These three functions, *leitourgia, martyria,* and *diakonia,* may be distinguished for the sake of a division of labor in the church, but never separated. If one of these functions is omitted, the fullness of the church's ministry in the world is diminished and may even cease to exist at all.

Diakonia without *leitourgia* would result in the transformation and degeneration of the service of love and compassion into social do-goodism and patronizing benevolence, and would be calculated by standards appealing to secular humanism and romantic idealism. Genuine ecclesial *diakonia* must be shaped in the crucible of worship and motivated by Word and sacraments. It seems clear that, whatever ministries deacons will be ordained to do in the world, they will and must assist pastors and bishops in the weekly Eucharist, which the Lima text calls "the central act of the Church's worship." Only in the closest *koinonia* with Christ can the church receive the power of the Spirit to love the unlovable and to resist in every way the demonization of the social conditions that distort life. There is a close connection between liturgical worship and social ministry.

Nor may *diakonia* be separated from *martyria,* the witness to Jesus, the Messiah of God and his people. A church which no longer witnesses to Jesus as the Savior of humankind has become nothing but a welfare agency. There is nothing wrong with a welfare agency, but it should not call itself "church," if that is not what it is. The diaconal action of the church is its energy flowing out from the body of Christ, going in the same direction as *agapē* love in the service of neighbors in need. In *agapē* love we serve persons for the sake of their need, not for ulterior reasons, such as to gain new recruits, build up the membership rolls, or get glamorizing publicity for the church. Love is not a technique to open doors.

Can the diaconal function of the church's ministry enjoy a comeback, along with the title of the deacon's office? Vatican II provided a stimulus to reform the office; the possibility for deacons to marry is one important step in the process. Another is to make it a perpetual office in its own right, and not a mere stepping-stone on the way to the priesthood.

Will American Lutheranism respond with favor to Lima's challenge to restore the diaconate in a credible and useful way? The church has become increasingly aware of the growing cleavage between itself and the world, even while the world around it is becoming religious and the church is becoming worldly. Many people, pastors as well as lay people, feel an almost insuperable gulf between Sunday piety and everyday existence. One way to overcome this cleavage is to build a diaconal bridge between what pastors do within the church and the life of the laity in the world. Will it work? How pragmatic do we need to be? The office was constituted by apostolic authority. It has had a zigzag history. But it is still alive and could enjoy a renewal today. Then perhaps seminarians, candidates for ordained ministry, would be given two options and not only the existing pastoral option, and thus be channeled into the church's cadres of service in accordance with their gifts and callings. We are now shoehorning into the pastoral niche persons whose qualifications do not fit the demands of the office.

We do need to recover the threefold pattern of ministry, not for the sake of our salvation but in order better to equip the church for its varied tasks. There are pastors without the gifts to be bishops, as there may be deacons without the gifts to be pastors. God has given a variety of gifts for a variety of services, and there is no reason for the church to continue to homogenize this apostolically ordained pattern of multiplicity.

9

The Pastoral Leader
in the Community of
Jesus Christ

The Communal Context of the Pastoral Office

The pastor is called and ordained to serve a community of persons elected by Jesus Christ. This predicate of the community is finally the only thing that distinguishes it from other kinds of social institutions. The community consists of individuals who have been called out of their many dark corners of the world to become "a chosen race, a royal priesthood, a holy nation, God's own people" (1 Peter 2:9). Belonging to a church is often seen as essentially no different than belonging to some other club, lodge, league, or guild. When we speak of the company of God's elect in Jesus Christ, we are not thinking of a group of like-minded people who enjoy keeping each other's company.

What we have already said about the *ecclesia* makes it an object of faith. *Credo ecclesiam!* I believe in the church. The hidden roots and the inner dynamics of this community grow out of its relationship to Jesus Christ, and none other. Otherwise, the church will be seen as a social fellowship for those who can afford it. Or the church will be seen as a religious clinic for those who need it, or as a social agency for idealistic persons who enjoy serving others, or as an ethical society for those who want to promote morals and manners, or as a useful civic organization to place the halo of religion on community projects, or as an educational institution to keep the children off the streets. A Christian community is free to involve itself in all sorts of educational, recreational, and charitable activities, but its *identity* is grounded solely in the transcendent datum of its election as the messianic community of the end-time, equipped with a revealed message and endowed with a universal mission to perform a sacrificial ministry as the representative of Christ for the world.

The new community is elected through the historical operations of the triune God. The full trinitarian basis of the church opens the community of Christ to the wider cosmic and eschatological dimensions of revelation and salvation. If the community belongs to Christ, it belongs also to the Father who sent him and to the Spirit who "calls, gathers, enlightens, and sanctifies the whole Christian church on earth and preserves it in union with Jesus Christ in the one true faith."[1] If we do not place the pastoral office within the context of the full contours of the church, based on the indivisible works of the Father, Son, and Holy Spirit, pastoral ministry tends to become closed in upon the self-interest of the community, concerned chiefly about its own spirituality and survival.

In light of the First Article of the Creed, the church represents the universal family of God, called forth out of the pluriform world which God created. The church is made of the secular stuff which God posited in creation; it never is changed into some supernatural, uncreated substance. There can thus be no question of a pastoral strategy that draws the church into isolation from the world, that pulls the veil of otherworldliness around its members, and severs itself from the cosmos of God's creation. The world is that which God saves, not that from which we are saved. "For God so loved the world. . ."!

In light of the Second Article of the Creed, the community is the place where the world is on the mend, where the deep miseries of the world are met by the still deeper mercies of God, where the alienated and the estranged learn to call the unfathomable mystery of the world by the name Jesus taught, ''Abba, Father!'' The community is the convocation of those who have responded to the summons of Christ to be his redemptive link to a world which he loves.

In light of the Third Article of the Creed, the church is the fellowship of the Holy Spirit, the communion of saints. The Holy Spirit is the power that actualizes the election of Jesus Christ, making individuals into a true community sharing the gifts of the Spirit, of which the most enduring is love. The Holy Spirit makes it possible for the community to fulfill its vocation of service in the world.

This trinitarian identity of the community of Jesus Christ allows us to understand the centripetal and centrifugal rhythm of the church. The church hears the evocative word of the Father and is called out of the world of many nations; the church is convoked in Christ, called together, gathered in the name of the crucified and risen Jesus; the church is sent with a vocation into the world, to be scattered as a spiritual disapora into every corner of the cosmos, counseled by the Spirit.

The transcendental datum of the community's identity is reinforced by the many biblical images which describe it. The community is elected to be the people of God, constituted by a mighty act of God's grace, beginning with Abraham, the father of a covenant community. The community is elected to be the body of the resurrected Christ, the corporate means of his own self-communication. The church is elected to be the bride of Christ, living in mutual love and fidelity. But often the church has played the whore, falling for other suitors, be they national identity, racial superiority, popular religion, partisan ideology, or other myths and isms. The church is elected to be the temple of the Holy Spirit, the place that God has elected to make his dwelling, replacing the old temple made of stone with a new one made of people. The church is elected to be the communion of saints, in which each member lives *with* every other (the principle of togetherness) and *for* every other (the principle of vicariousness).

The nature and functions of the pastoral office can not be properly defined without a theological description of the nature and attributes of the community which the pastor serves. Pastor and community go together; one cannot exist without the other, any more than the head can live without the body, or vice versa. We believe that the church is marked by attributes, the manifestation of which the pastor is called upon to serve. The church is one, holy, catholic, and apostolic. These are far-reaching qualities that determine the style of pastoral vocation.

The unity of the church is Jesus Christ himself. The pastor is the ecumenical leader of the local community, regarding every movement to fracture the unity of the body as an attack upon Christ. The pastor must so speak and act as to witness to only *one* God, *one* incarnation, *one* atonement, *one* gospel, *one* faith, *one* Baptism, and *one* Table of the Lord. A ministry oriented to the true unity of the church will locate its source in Christ alone and not trust in organizational manipulation, doctrinal compromise, religious relativism, or humanitarian good will.

The holiness of the church is one of election; it does not emanate from the virtuous lives of its members and leaders. Being elected unto holiness means being set apart for a special service in the world. Precisely because we share the reality of Christ by grace, we are being hallowed by the indwelling presence of the Holy Spirit, embodying this new state of being in a concrete style of life. Pastors are asked to play a leadership role in the service of holiness. "Take heed to yourselves and to all the flock, in which the Holy Spirit has made you overseers" (Acts 20:28). "Now a bishop must be above reproach, married only once, temperate, sensible, dignified, hospitable, an apt teacher, no drunkard, not violent but gentle, not quarrelsome, and no lover of money" (1 Tim. 3:2-3, RSV adapted). "For a bishop, as God's steward, must be blameless; he must not be arrogant or quick-tempered or a drunkard or violent or greedy for gain, but hospitable, a lover of goodness, master of himself, upright, holy, and self-controlled" (Titus 1:7-8). "Tend the flock of God that is your charge, not by constraint but willingly, not for shameful gain but eagerly, not as domineering over those in your charge but being examples to the flock" (1 Peter 5:2-3). These are only a few of the verses addressed to the pastoral leaders of early Christian congregations. The fact that these words had to be written in such forceful terms indicates that some things do not change, that leaders then were subject to the same character faults, moral failings, depraved conduct, and degrading habits that characterize many pastors of today's congregations. Pastors often complain that they are being measured by a double standard. Of course, this is not true. Pastors are only being asked as leaders to measure up to the same standard by which all Christians are to be judged. There is nothing in these apostolic injunctions that does not apply in principle to all baptized believers. A pastor's effectiveness stands or falls with the consistency by which these apostolic guidelines are cheerfully exhibited. The alternative is a ministry flawed by conformity to the world, compromise with the spirit of the age, and prophetic sluggishness.

The catholicity of the church refers to the universal scope of its life and mission, geographically in space and historically in time. Today this means that pastoral leadership will be both ecologically sensitive to the whole natural environment of human life and ecumenically open to the fullness of the catholic tradition. "Catholic" comes from the Greek *kata holos,* meaning "completely whole," the same root as in "holistic." A catholic style of leadership spells concern for the whole gospel for the whole mission for the whole world. It calls for catholicity in depth and breadth. Catholicity in depth means to express the fullness of the church and all the gifts of the Spirit. It means integrity and wholeness of tradition. Catholicity in breadth means to express the comprehensiveness of the saving purpose of God, the horizons of which reach to the very boundaries of creation itself. The whole world appears within the vision of the church. The love of God in Christ is universal. The ecumenical church reaches the whole inhabited world (*oikoumene*), going in all directions to the ends of the earth, bringing light and leaven into all the various racial, cultural, political, and economic forms of human life.

The apostolicity of the church has been the major theme of this book on mission and ministry. The decision for or against apostolicity determines whether the church is built on the sinking sand of passing human wisdom or on the granite foundation of the unsurpassable foolishness of God in Jesus Christ. Apostolicity means deciding what is healthy and unhealthy in the one, holy, catholic church by the criterion of the apostolic witness to Christ. The validity of the scripture principle is based on its connection with the apostolic word and witness. It is not enhanced by intramural squabblings about verbal inerrancy, nor is it refuted by extraecclesial pronouncements about historical relativism. The apostolic witness guarantees the identity of the church through the discontinuity of the times. Apostolicity is grounded in a succession of sendings: the Son by the Father, the Spirit by the Son, and the apostolic community by the triune God, all of which is documented in the New Testament canon and in the whole of the apostolic tradition. Therefore, the church must conform to the Scriptures, because they are the record of the prophetic and apostolic proclamation which the Spirit brought into conformity with the mind of Jesus Christ. The pastoral leader will be steeped in Scripture, knowing that the church cannot be holy, adhere to the gospel, and be subject to the lordship of Christ, if it lives in contradiction to the witness of the Scriptures. Many ecumenically minded Christians are enthusiastic about the quest for the unity of the church. Equally important is the concern of evangelically minded Christians who contend for the purity of the faith. It is the task of the leader to press for the ongoing renewal of faith and reform of doctrine by the Christ-centered criterion of apostolicity.

Preaching the Whole Counsel of God

The heart of the Christian faith is the *kerygma* of the dying and rising of Jesus, the Christ of God. Today some modern folk, a few with impressive theological credentials, regard this message of the dying and rising of Christ as a mythological shell of primitive Christianity, which we today with sophisticated hermeneutical scalpels can strip away to get at the inner nut, which happens to be a certain understanding of ourselves and a certain way of being in the world. The reverse is actually the case. The message of the dying and rising of Jesus the Messiah is not the mythic part of Christianity. It is the ontological-historical truth. What is mythological overgrowth is rather all the theories, explanations, rationalizations, and moralizations developed as substitutes for the hard core of historical revelation. The apostles who encountered the crucified and risen Jesus entered into the depths of reality. Ultimate reality was unveiled before their eyes, and they began to overthrow the cherished myths of their age. A reversal of the common opinion about truth and reality occurred. Ultimate reality was disclosed to them in the person of the dying and rising Messiah Jesus, who summed up in himself all truth—the truth of God, the truth of human nature, the truth of salvation, and the truth of the world's destiny. From now on, only that is real and true which points to Christ and finds meaning and completeness in him.

The community of Jesus Christ lives from this message. The solemn task of the pastoral leader is to be its primary medium of communication, so that it can be heard and heeded.

The New Testament word *kerygma* has basically two meanings. It means, first, the content of what is to be preached, and second, the act of preaching itself. In preaching today we must insist on the interdependence of content and act. The act without content is empty, and the content without act is dead. If the right content of preaching is not present, one cannot rescue the situation by rhetorical skill, though it often seems to help.

The community lives by listening. People who bother to come to church are there to listen, to get tuned in on the news, to hear the announcement of God's victory in their world. Only when they listen to the message of *Christus Victor* can they respond in thanksgiving and service. Therefore, we hold to the primacy of the Word and the means of grace. The community that assembles must come with ears cocked, before it can disperse to do the truth. So it was in the apostolic community. It was a listening community where the kerygma was proclaimed, both in the work of building up the community and in that of evangelistic outreach. What is this kerygma? It is the announcement of God's self-characterization in the personal life and ministry and in the cross and resurrection of Jesus the Christ. The Old Testament, too, played a part in this central event. The apostolic community saw this event as the fulfillment of the Old Testament promise of a Messiah to liberate Israel and establish the reign of God. The content of the kerygma is that this man Jesus, who was crucified, God has made to be Lord, that the prince of life who was killed has been raised from the dead. If that is not the center of the message we deliver in our congregations, we are not being faithful to our calling. Then we are dumping on people a pile of religious jargon or pious piffle on which they have overdosed already.

Preaching calls for listening to the voice of the living Christ who has entered into solidarity with the sick and suffering body of humanity and who speaks within it the creative word of life in his resurrected body. The message of the cross and resurrection is not only telling what God did once upon a time. That would make it like a fairy tale. That is the way we preach when we forget to believe. There is a place for telling stories, of course. Stories may be engaging, certainly more interesting than abstract theorizing about the world, the human condition, and divine things in general. However, sound preaching should not be delivered in the key of fairy-story telling, of what happened once upon a time and of living happily ever after. The sermon is not to become an occasion for a compulsive urge to entertain people with catchy stories, neither ours nor anyone else's. Anyway, stories both biblical and modern can also get stale through overrecitation. Some of the popular story-telling preachers, I am told, hire secretaries to go through books, articles, and human interest rag-sheets, clipping out cute stories about Johnny and Suzie to illustrate some moralizing platitudes.

But we do have a story to tell the people, God's story about the death and resurrection of his Messiah in the context of our human suffering and sickness unto death. God, through the gospel, is speaking and holding conversation with our listeners, telling them about God's struggles and sufferings in the death and resurrection of Jesus, about his death and victory in the real world of everyday life, about God's involvement, not in some far-off supernatural world to which we are being asked to ascend by means of spiritual gymnastics, but in the concrete lives of the hearers of the Word, "in all its detail and mistake and humor and fatigue and surprise and contradiction and freedom and ambiguity and quiet and wonder and sin and peace and vanity and variety and lust and triumph and defeat and rest and love and all the rest that it is from time to time."[2] This crucified and risen Messiah who lives in the Word is God's way of entering into our world, determining the destiny of the nations, tangling with the principalities and powers, calling upon the constellation of authorities—the universities, corporations, political parties, unions, and all others with power—to serve the people. The Word is a two-edged sword, putting down the oppressors from their seats of power, and exalting those of low degree.

If the meaning of the biblical message is faithfully expounded, we will not have to resort to gimmickry to make it relevant for today. When we address the kerygma of the living Christ to the listener, we are speaking of an event that is intrinsically relevant and potentially a turning point in every person's existence. Many pastors preach as though they do not expect anything to happen. They have contracted the disease of the age. The slogan is that deeds and not words count in this revolutionary age of rapid change. There is truth in this impression. We can hardly deny that the apostolic kerygma has been drowned out by evangelistic verbosity and monological pomposity.

The strength of the church lies in its weakness. Its only power lies in its communicative word, not in a role of power broker amidst the superpowers of the world. Efforts to renew the church by the wisdom of the world are doomed to failure. The kerygma brings the promise of life; the law breeds death. The law that the church shall live according to legalistic prescriptions about quotas will lead to the death of the church. Change in the church depends on preaching the whole counsel of God. The law leads to indictment; only the gospel can create the conditions of renewal that spell a new day for the church. Every proposal for the renewal of the church that does not take its point of departure, orientation, and motivation from the kerygma of the death and resurrection of Christ will bring not new life but decadence to the church. We must keep this axiom firmly in mind. The church can be renewed only by the events which created its life in the first place. What created the church was the apostolic witness to the cross and resurrection of Jesus the Christ. In Lutheran terminology, this message is composed of both law and gospel, both negation and newness.

What Luther meant by law and gospel is what recent biblical theology sees as the kerygma of the crucified and risen Jesus Christ. For Luther the Bible did nothing else than preach Christ under the aspects of law and gospel, death and resurrection. What is to be preached is to be heard, and cannot be seen. "Stick your eyes in your ears," Luther said. "He who will not take hold with his ears but wants to look with his eyes is lost."[3]

There are several tendencies in the church that threaten to cut the lifeline of the community's listening to the Word. (1) The first is the failure of faith. Is Christ himself actively proclaiming himself through the contemporary word of preaching? Does God really speak to us today in the living word? If we have doubts about that, perhaps we are among those who look upon the book as a good substitute for the *viva vox*. Perhaps Christ is a prisoner of Scripture, locked up in the box of the Bible. Then we would have a dead Christ whose obituary is the Bible. (2) Others lock Christ up in the dogmas or confessions of the church. The content of preaching is so important that perhaps we are unwilling to leave anything to the imagination of the preacher and the impulse of the Spirit. So preaching becomes a recitation of the dogmatic contents of past preaching, and salvation comes by believing in a sacred minimum of propositional truths. Biblicism and confessionalism are both dangerous tendencies, particularly appealing when the church is going through times of rapid change. When the kerygma is not understood as the action of God in the human realm of sin and suffering, guilt and anxiety, despair and death, in the dying and rising of Jesus the Christ, the kerygma is transmuted into historical facts, doctrinal truths, or edifying discourses. The result is homocentric religion and piety. Then we think of the kerygma as essentially raw material for *our* reflection and meditation, and for the cultivation of *our* religious and moral personalities.

The kerygma is first the action of God in the death and resurrection of Christ, and second the representation of this event as a living word of divine self-communication today. As the real Christ is the real baby lying in real straw in a real manger, he is equally real and livingly present as the crucified and resurrected Christ in our real human words. The kerygma is not the voice of God crying out once upon a time; it is the living word of God crying out his peace and blessings over the bloody body of dying humanity. True preaching is God's summons, the act of addressing listeners in their real situation, unveiling the Christ who forgives and heals, who struggles and conquers, who raises up and makes alive. If we believed this in our preaching, we would sweat blood preparing our sermons. The true task of preaching is to become the rendezvous where Christ and sinners meet. Preaching is Christ coming into his own world to announce the victory which he achieved through conflict and death, on Golgotha and in the grave. Preaching is the link between the resurrection hope of Jesus Christ and the dying of every person in the world.

How sad it is for the church to be retarded by preachers who do not take preaching seriously. Some pastors have given up hope in the pulpit for trust in the magic of the altar. The priestly posture and not the prophetic posture, the praying church and not the listening church are seen as portraying the authentic relation between the Word of God and human beings. I do not wish to suggest that this is an either/or. But some have made it that. The liturgy is expected to compensate for a dreadful homily.

If the pastor is not a liturgical specialist, perhaps he or she is prepared to editorialize the congregation on the latest events. To be sure, the preacher will stress social concerns, the church being a leaven in society. Here too the Word must have priority. Before the community is scattered to do the truth, to live the Word in the world, it must be gathered for a real hearing. Otherwise, the church will bring no difference to bear on the world. The temptation is for preachers to recycle what the world dreams up. In hearing a sermon, a congregation has the right to ask: Is what is being said equally valid apart from the death and resurrection of Christ? Is the living word of Christ the absolute condition of the truth of what is being proclaimed? Would one have to be a believer in Christ and a member of his community to be saying the things this preacher is taking his time and mine to be saying?

Homiletics must be taught in seminaries on the basis of a sound biblical and theological hermeneutic. Together they must answer: How can we preach the death and resurrection of Christ in such a way that people will be brought to a real hearing of the Word? But a note of caution is in order. Our insistence on the hermeneutical significance of the death and resurrection of Christ does not mean we preach only those passages in the Bible that speak explicitly of the double ending of his life. The cross and resurrection form the center of gravity of the New Testament portrayal of the life of Jesus of Nazareth and provide the condition for a true interpretation of the meaning of the kingdom he established. If Christ is the center, there is also a circumference of the biblical world of meaning. The Bible as a whole must come into play. We are not Marcionites who preach a part of the New Testament to the exclusion of God's preparatory revelation in the Old Testament. Nor are we Gnostics who pick and choose the more lofty insights of Scripture that appeal to the spiritually elite. So we preach the whole counsel of God from alpha to omega. We preach all the acts of God from creation to the eschaton. We preach the acts of God in the Old Testament, as those who stand within the horizon of the new covenant. We preach from within an ecclesial framework. The series of events attested in the Old and New Testaments as well as the series of events running up to our present time and indeed into the unknown future are interconnected by a link. The link is the cross and resurrection of Jesus, without which there is no gospel, no kerygma, and in fact no church of Christ. Without it we lose the unity of the whole chain of mighty acts of God. Then our preaching is driven by the winds of current fads and the hot air of personal whim. The times and the self become overinflated. Instead of sharing the whole counsel of God we offer sentimental autobiography, two-bit psychology, pietistic effusions, and unedifying dogmatizing. The whole Bible is dealing with God's conquest of demonic forces that enslave humankind. The whole drama of salvation is encapsulated in the conflict and victory of the cross and resurrection of Jesus Christ. It holds within itself universal meaning and eschatological hope for humanity and the world.

Presiding at the People's Liturgy

The New Testament word for ministry is *diakonia*. Its secular meaning was "to wait on tables." This is a large part of the work of the ministry, serving at the Table of the Lord and leading the *leitourgia*. The word *liturgy* comes from the two Greek words, *leitos,* meaning "public," and *ergon,* meaning "work." In its secular sense *leitourgia* is a public service rendered by a citizen at his or her own expense. In the New Testament it comes to mean presiding at the public service of the people. This gives us a clue that worship does not consist only of what we say but also of what we do. Liturgy is the work of the people of God. It is the kind of praxis that precedes the social expressions of love in action.

Since the first century, believers in Christ and members of his church have gathered every week around the Table of the Lord as one fellowship, eating and drinking with Jesus and expressing their visible unity in one body. The Lima text on "Baptism, Eucharist and Ministry" calls the celebration of Holy Communion "the central act of the church's worship."[4] The liturgy is a form of drama. The word *drama* means "deed," something done. Dramatic liturgy reflects our belief in how God reveals himself in the world. Theology now emphasizes that in the biblical sense revelation is historical. The Bible is the revealing record of the history of God's works of salvation. The German word *Heilsgeschichte* has entered into common theological parlance. It means the "history of salvation." Revelation comes to us in the drama of history, and so is recapitulated in the liturgy of worship.

We have already said that preaching is the representation of the saving acts of God, interweaving them with the warp and woof of our daily existence. In preaching, we rehearse the mighty deeds of redemption, first at the Red Sea, where the Israelites go down and come up, second, in the person of Jesus Christ who goes down into the grave and comes up in new life, and third, in our existence when the "old ego" is drowned in the waters of Baptism and a new self comes forth and rises up.[5]

The impression is widespread that the results of the liturgical renewal movement are too prettified and elitist to be of much use to the masses. The liturgical movement in the nature of the case has been in the hands of an elite minority. They have done an excellent work in linking the liturgy to the pole of Scripture and tradition. But communication is a two-way street. The pole of contemporaneity has been short-circuited. If liturgy has little or nothing to do with the common life of the people, it is a failure, no matter how biblical or beautiful. All the traditional language of the liturgy was modern once upon a time. No language, set of symbols, or gestures have descended from heaven. They are all culturally conditioned. Liturgy thus moves between two poles: the historically revelational and the culturally relational. The content of the liturgy must be a dramatic representation of the acts of God in history, but the form of our liturgy must be a medium in which people express the sounds and songs of their hearts. Liturgical worship must be biblical and it must be popular, reflecting the rich variety of racial, social, emotional, and educational experiences of modern-day people. The liturgical style that fits the saints that gather in the Midwest chapels of St. Olaf, Wittenberg, and Valparaiso will scarcely be suited to a majority of Blacks, Chicanos, and Indians, and perhaps not even to the sons and daughters of the older generation that sends its children there. Lutherans have moved from a red book to a green book of worship on the assumption that one liturgical style can automatically be indigenized in every kind of sociological setting. In a curious way liturgy must express not only what we believe about God but also what we feel about ourselves. This cannot be expressed in a set of categories and symbols alien to the ordinary social contexts and cultural patterns of our pluralistic world. The church must recover the apostolic *ésprit de finesse* to become in its liturgy as a Jew to the Jews, barbarian to the barbarians, Chinese to the Chinese, Indian to the Indians, to become all things to all peoples, that none shall be excluded from the church's worship of God.

The theological basis for constructing a liturgy that dialectically relates the biblical-revelational and contemporary-cultural poles of the divine-human encounter in worship is given in the classical doctrine of the Trinity.

Liturgy testifies to God the creator, when our worship uses the common material and natural things of the world to signify that all things have their origin in God and are therefore good. There is no original split between the sacred and the secular. Unfortunately, the tendency of the church has been to change ordinary things to look extraordinary, to supernaturalize them, to cover them with an ecclesiastical glow and religious veneer, and thus to sever their continuity with the natural things of this God-created world. Hence, the church has traditionally used a special ecclesiastical bread which does not look like ordinary bread at all. In recent years, one finds real bread being broken on the altars, and that is symbolically a gain. It symbolizes that God chooses the natural things of this earth—things like water, bread, wine, and oil—as vessels used in proclaiming the presence of God.

Liturgy should also testify that, though God created this world very good, it has become disfigured, and that, in spite of this, God has chosen to mend it. Our liturgical action should make transparently clear that the fallen world is being redemptively transformed, but never transubstantiated. Water remains water, bread and wine remain bread and wine, though they are now drawn into a special redemptive context.

Liturgy should also testify that God is sanctifier, that the broken and disrupted relations between human beings are being healed and restored to a truly personalized community. God as Spirit deals with us as persons destined for freedom, not by means of tyrannical power but through personal presence.

The story of God's self-incarnation has broken down the wall of separation between the holy and the common. The wall has been erected again and again by priests and pastors in the Christian tradition. The sanctuary has become insulated from the world. The tragic effect of drawing a veil around supposedly sacred things and cutting off the secular is that the powers of redemption get bottled up, rather than being released into the world where they ought to go. When the holy becomes a small circle in the world—a self-enclosed nucleus—the bridges from the church to the world break down, and both the church and the world are losers.

Israel had a tremendous sense of the holiness and transcendence of God. This was symbolized by its "holy of holies" and its great fear of vocalizing the proper name of God. The Christian faith also knows of the holy transcendence of God, but the unique thing is that God's holy transcendence has become lowly immanence, exhibited not in a segregated and inaccessible tabernacle but in the simplicity of a quite accessible stable. The familiar, ordinary, common, run-of-the-mill things of this world take on special significance when the real presence of God is manifest not in a religious corner of the world, but in the midst of public things. The cocoon of religion could not hold Jesus Christ. He goes out into the open of God's world, refusing to be closeted up in a world of religious professionals.

Theological Education for the Teaching Ministry

Modern New Testament scholarship has refined for us the basic distinction in apostolic Christianity between *kerygma* and *didache*. It was Martin Dibelius, cofounder with Rudolf Bultmann of the form-critical school, who formulated the slogan: "In the beginning was the kerygma." The earliest Christian activity was the preaching of the kerygma. We have followed this apostolic sense of priorities by insisting on the priority of the kerygma in the existence of the church, over worship, teaching, and service. We have opted for a mission paradigm of the meaning of ministry. The preaching of the kerygma declares God's word and will and work of reconciliation in Jesus Christ. Only on that basis can we worship and teach and serve in the name of Jesus. Precisely because God is active in the totality of our life, we cannot lend his Word only our ears. A total response is being evoked from us. Our hearts in worship, our minds in teaching, and our hands in service combine to echo the Word of God in our ears.

The apostle Paul said, "It pleased God by the foolishness of the *kerygmatos* to save them that believe" (1 Cor. 1:21). But Paul did not only preach that people might believe. He also taught believers that they might understand and be weaned from milk to eat solid food. *Kerygma* leads to *didache*. Preaching must be followed up by teaching in order that understanding might lead to witness. Those whom Jesus called were disciples before they became apostles. The upbuilding, the *oikodome,* of the community in the New Testament requires this preaching-teaching sequence. Faith suffocates when it does not reach the level of understanding.

Those who are called must be instructed before being ordained. The ordained person is a successor of the apostle, one who is sent on a mission with a message. But such a one must first be schooled in the discipline of the Master. The kerygma as the subject of preaching soon becomes the object of teaching. The New Testament itself is the record of this continual, dynamic transition from preaching to teaching. The subject matter of Christian teaching is "the faith which was once for all delivered to the saints" (Jude 3). The Greek word *paradosis* means "tradition." The Greek verb *paradidonai* means "to hand down" or "to deliver." The word which was preached did not disappear into thin air. It became the starting point of teaching; it was incorporated into a body of tradition. This body of tradition grew and expanded and became a deposit of teaching for the whole church. The early tradition entered a process of development under the guidance of the Holy Spirit, bringing to the community's remembrance the meaning of the salvation events within the horizon of ever new situations and challenges. The traditioning process began already in the first century, even in the writing of the four Gospels. The Gospels are neither pure *kerygma* nor mere *history,* but a mixture of reports of historical events in the life of Jesus and soteriological interpretations of them in the life of the church, resulting in an ecclesially shaped picture of the historical Jesus as the eschatological Christ. Form criticism has made us irrefutably aware of this interweaving of fact and interpretation in the Gospels. These Gospels, like the Epistles and the other New Testament writings, became the embryonic tradition of the missionary church. In due course of time they became the church's canon of right teaching, the foundational documents of the church's faith, and the pericopes for the preaching that perpetuates the life of the church.

The reason the kerygma gave rise to a teaching tradition is that true faith which responds to the gospel of Christ has within its structure the element of knowing. Theology as the work of the intellect inheres in the nature of faith to seek fuller understanding. In the Gospel of John "knowing" and "believing" are used interchangeably. One cannot believe what one does not in some sense know. Paul went into detailed theological exposition in Galatians and Romans both because he encountered misunderstanding in those communities and because he wanted them to grow in certainty. The Christian answer to problems of faith cannot be "only believe." There must also be wisdom, insight, knowledge, and understanding. The statements of the kerygma and of the developing *paradosis* call for fresh interpretations in new situations. In this dialectic of questions and answers we find the beginnings of theology as we know it. The early church did not develop in a vacuum. It was challenged to express its identity within a syncretistic context of competing religions and philosophies, creating the risk that teachers of the new faith would compromise its integrity to make it more palatable. There were the Judaizers who looked upon Christ as a second Moses, and the Gnostics who believed he was a phantasmal figure and not a real human being. The church found many shifting winds of doctrine blowing in the communities. There were false apostles, false prophets, false teachers, conveying a pseudogospel. Many of the latest writings in the New Testament show a great deal of concern over false teachers—for example, the Pastoral Epistles, Jude, Revelation, and 2 Peter. They found that babes in the faith must be warned against the seductions of the "elemental spirits of the universe." The life of the church is continually threatened by heresy. Heresy is a fundamental option of believing and thinking that cuts the links to the teaching of the apostles concerning Christ.

The church's concern for true doctrine gave rise to its concern for effective authority. What is the final court of appeal when there are differences of doctrine and conflicts that divide the body? Who is to say who is right? Of course, they all said, Christ the Lord is the authority, and so those who knew him—the apostles—held a place of preeminence as his personally appointed representatives. After them, then who? There was plenty of maneuvering for the right to appeal to "the apostles of our Lord Jesus Christ." There is no way to Jesus Christ around the apostles. The growing tradition had to be rooted in the apostolic tradition. Thus it is significant that the first manual of ethics and instructions in the church was given the title "The Teaching of the Twelve Apostles." This is the famous *Didache,* forgotten for over a thousand years and rediscovered in 1873.

Three things happened as ways of settling disputes about the right to appeal to the apostles. First, the bishops were increasingly given a special kind of authority. By common conviction they were the successors of the apostles, hence the authorized bearers of the oral tradition. Second, as the oral traditions were written down, they were ascribed to the apostles, some of them even to the disciples. Third, in this quandary about which of all the new writings accredited to the apostles were "authentic," a selection was made and the canon was crystallized. A fourth stage in answer to the question of authority developed when bishops of rival sees fell into conflict on fundamental teachings. Thus synods or councils of the church were convoked, producing creeds which became normative interpretations of the faith.

There we have the rudiments of the teaching authority of the old catholic church. A final capstone in the whole development was the increasing authority of the bishop of Rome, whose office claimed primacy by virtue of being in succession to Peter.

Ordained ministers of the gospel are custodians of the apostolic tradition. A few who have studied for an advanced degree in theology are called "Dr." *Doctor* comes from the Latin *docere,* which means "to teach." A *doctor ecclesiae* is a teacher of the church. A minister of the church should be called "Dr." as a title not of personal honor but of vocational function. Medical practitioners are called "Dr." because they used to teach; now they operate and prescribe drugs. There is not much we can do about distorted language. But we can take care that we lift up the teaching function of the pastoral office.

Jesus was called "rabbi." This title better conveys the teaching role of the minister of Jesus Christ than does "doctor" in our society. But it has come to be reserved exclusively for ordained Jewish ministers. Shall we call ministers "theologians"? At theological conferences and synod meetings pastors will often take the mike and introduce what they have to say with the words, "I am not a theologian but. . . ." Such persons have presumably studied theology for at least four years to get a Master of Divinity degree. The word *Master* was traditionally bestowed on individuals who had passed the examination of their peers in a particular field of study, and were thereby licensed to teach. Can one imagine persons who have achieved a degree in law rising to their feet and addressing the court, "I am not a lawyer but. . ."? Would not such persons lose all credibility before the judge and the jury? But when it comes to ministers, one occasionally hears, "He's a good pastor, but he's no theologian." Theologians are supposed to be persons who have gone on to graduate school, written a thesis, and acquired a doctorate. Any clear-eyed observer should know, however, that graduate schools are now mostly centers for the scientific study of religion, all of which has almost nothing to do with making a person a theologian, a teacher of the church.

The church has traditionally prepared its candidates for the ordained ministry in seminaries. In recent times Protestant churches in America have lowered their standards and have begun to accept candidates who have taken their degrees from university programs of religious studies. The question is whether the university can be expected to teach the theology that the church requires for the preparation of its ordained ministry. Paul Tillich opened his *Systematic Theology* with the statement: "Theology is a function of the church."[6] In Europe, theological faculties exist in state universities, but this is left over from a past arrangement between church and state. As the process of secularization speeds up, the pattern will inevitably change. In the United States the universities have become radically secularized, with very few exceptions. What kind of theology can they teach? A university can provide a setting for the scientific study of religion from the critical perspectives of history, phenomenology, philosophy, psychology, or sociology. Some universities are now fielding impressive religious studies programs, all under the rubric of the scientific study of religion. We would have to have lost our sense of the apostolic tradition in the church to believe that religious studies of this kind can provide a curricular core capable of educating persons for the ordained ministry. This belief is based on the illusion that theology is mostly concerned about religion and religious things, only more so. We should remind ourselves of what William Temple once said: "God is not particularly interested in religion." Nor were Jesus and the apostles in the business of pushing religion.

How can the church expect its clergy to be properly educated for ministry in a modern secular university, subject to no system of authority acknowledged by the church, neither Scripture, church tradition, creeds, confessions, synods, councils, offices, nor anything linked specifically to the teaching of the apostles? As long as Christian theology is bound to the revelation of God in Jesus Christ according to the apostolic tradition, there will be an ecclesial condition in the doing of theology for ministry that cannot be adequately satisfied in the context of a university department of religious studies, even if it should anachronistically call itself a "divinity school." The university can and should deal with all the knowledge available to human reason on its own. Theology is an ecclesial science that deals with the presuppositions, contents, and implications of the knowledge of divine revelation which "flesh and blood" have not disclosed to us (Matt. 16:17). As things stand today, departments of religious studies are among the worst possible places one can imagine to educate the mind and heart for the ministry given to the gospel of Word and sacraments. Theologians who teach theology in a secular university under some other guise realize that for the majority of their secular colleagues, theology does not really belong alongside medicine, law, and business, but more in a class with astrology, palmistry, and necromancy. Many Christians who teach a discipline in a secular university do so as "anonymous atheists," that is, proceeding for all practical purposes on the premise that "God is dead."

What is the difference in the study of theology for ministry in a seminary context? The difference is that theology in the seminary starts with the historical self-revelation of the God of Israel through Jesus Christ to the whole world, and then moves outward to inquire into the relation of this particular knowledge to what can be known of God from the common experience of human life in the world. Theology starts with the Word of God within the context of a confessing community, open to the infinite horizon of its meaning in relation to all other mediations of meaning through reason, nature, history, and experience. The difference has to do with the starting point, the curricular core, and the mission purpose which orients the study of theology.

The difference is decisive when it comes to the preparation of candidates for the ordained ministry of the church. Teachers of the church do theology for the sake of the gospel's mission and the church's ministry. Professors of theology are "called and ordained" as servants of the Word, living and teaching under the church's discipline. The seminary is the place where theology consciously moves from the sources of the gospel to the fields of ministry. Theology is not done for theology's sake, but to clarify the identity of the apostolic gospel of Jesus Christ under the conditions of the church's encounter with the modern world.

An ordained pastor is the church's theologian in a local congregation. As a teacher of the apostolic tradition, the pastor is committed to the confessional norms of the whole catholic church. They are applicable in every aspect of teaching. These norms are the three *sola*s articulated, but certainly not invented, at the time of the Reformation: *sola scriptura, sola gratia,* and *sola fide.* All three of these exist for the sake of the *solus Christus* (Chapter 2). The pastor performs a teaching service within a fellowship founded on truth and seeking fuller understanding. Truth is an eventful encounter between the Word of God and human existence in the world. We need to keep asking ourselves whether our teaching is the truth revealed in Jesus, the *aletheia.* We need to beware lest our teaching become trapped in the illusions of the age. We need to practice what Paul Ricoeur has called a "hermeneutics of suspicion," raising serious questions about truth and error in the church's preaching, teaching, and mission. We must, above all, become students of the Scriptures, so that we can see things as did the prophets and apostles, who viewed all things in the light of Jesus Christ. We need, as Karl Barth said, eyes of faith like "the cat's eyes that see in the dark."

Toward a Recovery of the Healing Ministry

There are signs that the church today is serious about recovering the healing dimension of ministry. Most candidates for ministry have studied pastoral care and counseling and have completed a basic requirement in Clinical Pastoral Education. This is an essential form of service both within and outside the church. From New Testament times the church has been committed to a ministry of healing. Our German Lutheran forebears called it *Seelsorge,* the care of souls. We must not think that the church has only in our time discovered the art of attending to the mental health of people. The prayer of the church is a healing action within the community.

Prayer is the openness of the self to the grace of God as the power source of healing. Gustaf Aulén, therefore, calls prayer a means of grace,[7] a third sacrament in addition to Baptism and the Lord's Supper. Prayer is not merely a human act of the self turning to God; it is at the same time a divine act by which God draws the self into his Spirit. Prayer is not only the quest of divine communion in love. It presupposes this communion and is an expression of the self being grasped by God's grace and love. There is no psychological substitute for the means which God has placed in the hands of believers, prayer in the name of Jesus. The name of Jesus is meant to prevent prayer from being used as a power in our control to manipulate God, or as a technique of autosuggestion or transcendental meditation by which we keep things under our control. Pastoral counseling becomes ineffective when it is predicated on humanistic psychology, which calls for the sick to heal themselves by gaining more self-knowledge. The power of the keys does not lie in magical trust in psychological words and theories about human behavior.

The pastor receives the power of the keys as a minister of the means of grace. This does not preclude the use of all available insights from psychology, psychiatry, and psychoanalysis. But these disciplines do not make the keys. The keys come from the promise of the Word and the power of the Spirit. They are placed in the hands of the stewards of the mysteries. There is a dimension of healing that goes beyond the medical and the psychotherapeutic. A person as a centered self is more than a collection of parts, more than a system of physical functions and more than a body of feelings. A person is spirit. And what is spirit? The spirit is the essential self. It is not another system of functions alongside the others. The spirit is not a fourth ''thing'' in addition to the physical, mental, and emotional aspects of life. The spirit is the central unity of them all. The spirit is the self that can say ''I myself,'' capable of being deeply self-reflexive, open to the world, to others, and to the infinite mystery of all reality. I use my mind, I control my emotions, and I develop my body. I am the center of them all, the principle of their meaning and purpose.

For this reason the pastoral counselor cannot have a specialization distinctly separate from the other members of the healing team. If the pastor's concern is the life of the spirit, that is a concern that integrates and embraces all the others. The minister of the gospel cannot stick to purely spiritual concerns, as though they operated in a separate compartment from the life of the body, the life of the mind, and the life of the emotions. The healer's concern is with the central meaning and unity of them all in a nonobjectifiable dimension.

In recent years numerous disciplines have converged on this notion that all aspects of our existence belong in an organic whole, and that we cannot effectively address a person as a mere composite of separate faculties. We must deal with each person as a whole— body, mind, and soul. Spirit is the name of that whole, the center of the self which lives in, with, and under all its different and distinguishable aspects.

Christian faith is a message of salvation for the person as a whole. Recent theology has coined the term ''holistic salvation.'' This term is based on the basic Christian affirmation that God became fully human: the Word of God has become human flesh and blood; the Spirit of God communicates to the human world through a human body. This means that every bone of our body, the movement of every muscle, every living cell of our brain, and the most delicate desires of our flesh have assumed spiritual meaning and purpose. This message of the incarnation is the basis of the kind of *Seelsorge* our laity have a right to expect of their pastors. Pastoral counselors will care for the person as a whole, enter into dialog in depth with the person, and release the energies of the Paraclete into every aspect of personal being.

Pastoral care has not always been what it should be. There are two great temptations, two ways of missing the mark in pastoral care.

The first way is to separate the spirit from the body and to settle for the life of the spirit apart from the body. This is the great spiritualistic misunderstanding of Christianity. Then the language of the pastor becomes spiritual, artificially pious, gaseous rhetoric about ghostlike subjects far removed from common human experience. Talk about salvation becomes a thing for the soul, nothing for the mind. But soul salvation is not whole salvation. Therefore it is not Christian salvation. It is a spiritualistic heresy.

The second temptation connected with the first is to gain the salvation of the soul at the expense of the body. The more you deny and punish the body, the more you build up a treasury of benefits for the soul in heaven.

There was an old Christian ascetic, Blessed Henry Suso, who wanted so badly to follow Christ that he denied the body to let the soul go free. For this reason he wore, as so many who wanted to become saints did in those days, a hair shirt and an iron chain around his body. He had someone make him a half-length, tight-fitting coarse undergarment, equipped with 150 sharp brass nails facing into the flesh. This was his nightshirt for 16 years. On hot summer nights, when he was half-dead from fatigue and bloodletting, he would fret and squirm sleeplessly from side to side like a worm being pricked with sharp needles. This is an extreme case of denying the body as a discipline for the soul. But it is wrong, not only as an extreme, but wrong from the beginning, to place the interests of the spiritual life against the body and make the body the enemy of the soul.

A Christian healer will not separate the spiritual from the psychic and the somatic aspects of life. We will not minister to the person to the neglect of the needs of the body and the hunger of the mind and the feelings of the soul. Maybe we will even be accused of meddling, of sticking our nose into the business of other specialists, each claiming a hold on one distinguishable aspect of the whole person. The minister's business is everybody's business. Although we cannot pretend to be amateur doctors and should not try to be pseudo-psychotherapists, we must give the gospel free course and let its effects flow into the bodily and mental states of the one who is sick. We do not claim to possess magical powers. But we bring a Word of healing that can touch the transcendental unity of life in the spirit which links all its dimensions into a whole person.

The governing idea of salvation and healing today is holistic. Health is wholeness. This is based on the Christian message that God was in Christ, a whole human person, that he came to bring life and salvation, to make people whole, to heal the sick, to be for every person the Great Physician, the master model of what it means to care for others, not merely as a way of making a living but as a

way of life, not as a job but as a calling, not for oneself but for
others. If a pastoral counselor exemplifies that model, it is bound
to cause some trouble. It is bound to bring judgment as well as
consolation. It will surely call into question many of our callous,
heartless, and self-serving practices in the care of sick and dying
people.

Paul Tournier, a medical doctor and a lay theologian, has said,
"Medicine has lost the sense of the person, the sense of man as a
whole."[8] He has promoted the idea of integrating medicine into a
ministry to the whole person. God help the sick person who falls
into the hands of specialists who take a piecemeal approach to the
body.

There is a crisis today in the field of professional health care. The
old saying, "Physician, heal thyself," is applicable. The very systems in our society that are to fight disease and promote health have
succumbed to a disease and, as Ivan Illich says, this disease has
reached epidemic proportions.[9] The church and its chaplains cannot
sit by and fiddle while others are taking the heat. Bear in mind, the
church does not have a minor stake in the field of health, for its
very concept of holistic salvation is intrinsically connected to health.
The promise of salvation gives us all certain inalienable rights.
Health is a concern of all the people. No group or association has
any right to a monopoly of control in this field. The idea of Christian
wholeness, of salvation, means that our people, all the people, have
a right to a strong and healthy body. That is not a privilege of the
rich who can afford to pay for it. That is something we as a collective
people, as a society, as a human community of persons, owe to each
other as a most solemn obligation that comes from the one Lord
God, the Maker and Savior of us all. Our people, all the people,
have a right to a strong and healthy imagination, a right to a strong
and healthy will, and a right to a strong and healthy spirit. The
church has recognized the totality of these claims in its history by
being intensely involved in schools and universities, by having been
the patron of the arts and sciences, by having led the way in founding
hospitals and other institutions of mercy. The church understands
the gospel as a movement in history to promote life and health. The
church must, therefore, participate today in the dialog that searches

for authentic norms of strength and health, of the body, emotions, reason, imagination, and will.

Finally, the role of the pastor goes beyond care and counseling for life here and now. The pastor is also called upon to be a chaplain bringing the message of eternal life in the dark hours of dying and grief when all other systems have failed. This is the meaning of the last rites and the anointing with oil. The pastor is often the last person in the room, and can bring a cheering word of hope in a hopeless situation. The Christian has a message of resurrected life beyond death, of ultimate hope against hope, of victory in the face of death. Dispensing the sacrament of eternal life, the medicine of immortality, as Ignatius put it, is the last and best ministry we have to offer in times of death and dying. The time comes when medical and psychological interventions become no longer useful, when to apply them even becomes sinful, when they can get in the way of a person's encounter with the symbols of eternal life in preparing to face death. In this time only the symbols of faith have power; only God's eschatological peace can pierce the fog of fear and dread in the face of death; only the message of the cross and resurrection can teach a person the graceful art of dying with courage and hope.

When it comes to dying, we are all amateurs. None of us has much experience, and none can boast of being good at it. We have this message from one who has gone before, one who has led the way into death to demystify it, to break its deadly grip on us, to forge a link to a future of resurrected life in which death has been put to death and peace shall reign for ever and ever.

Servants of the Servants of God

The pastor is a leader of a community that exists for the world, for every person in every place in every time. When the community lives close to Jesus Christ, it lives close to the world, following the lead of its Master who laid down his life for others. Discipleship under Christ equals stewardship in the world. The turning of God toward the world in the Christ event determines the fundamental orientation of the community. The place for the church is in the world, finding ways to serve its needs.

Preaching, teaching, presiding, counseling, and overseeing the life of the congregation is more than a full-time job. We have already referred to the minister's dilemma, the maceration of the minister, the crisis of ministry today, compounded by the sheer multiplicity of functions that drive a person in too many directions at once. How then do we dare to place an additional burden of responsibility on the minister as leader of the servants of God in the world? The answer is that the church's mission of evangelization, diaconic work, and social criticism must be carried on by all the believers. The ministry of Word and sacraments to the community aims to equip the whole church for stewardship in the world. The pastor's ministry is to the community, and the community's is to the world. If the community is to serve, it must first be equipped through preaching and teaching. The church is tempted to think of itself as an end in itself rather than as a means to an end—the end of God's total mission for the entire cosmos. The goal of the church's existence is not to secure its own salvation but to share the word of cosmic redemption. It is unrealistic to expect ordained pastors to be the primary points of contact between the church and the world. It is sufficient for them to release the enormous potential of the laity for its ministry within the structures of the world.

We have already developed a theology of mission and evangelization for the whole church in today's world, and we have called for a restoration of the diaconate as a ministry of love in action to the poor and the needy who eke out a substandard existence at the margins. The local congregation is an outpost of evangelistic and diaconic service. The pastor is like the drill sergeant preparing the troops for battle, working more often on the base than on the front-lines of duty. I am not enchanted by this military image, although the New Testament is full of it. But it does create a picture that fits the ministry. The real shock troops are the laity. The universal priesthood of all believers is not intended to be an attack on the place of the ordained clergy within the church. The fight is not clergy versus laity. The battle is in the world, pastors equipping laity for their ministries. The laity are over 99% of the total membership of the church. What if they all became pressed into the service of the *ecclesia militans*? Hendrik Kraemer referred to the laity as the "frozen assets" of the church.[10] They are the pioneers of the mission on the outposts of the church. It is simply wrongheaded to expect pastors to be in as many places doing evangelism and service as the laity. The pastoral task is to work for the integration of the laity into the being and mission of the church. The laity have rights and they have duties. They are the vanguard of the mission of the church, for they already work in places where ordained persons cannot normally freely move. If the laity do not penetrate deeply into the secular spheres of life, the church will be without a voice in those places.

When laity are challenged to do church work, it usually comes in the form of a sermon for "Stewardship Sunday" dealing with the triad of time, talents, and treasures. An outstanding layperson is one who gives a lot of money to the church, serves on various committees, or moves up the ecclesiastical ladder and gets involved in other programs of sterile inbreeding. These lay people who have mastered the techniques of being "good Christians" in church are very visible. Pastors quite naturally depend on them. But this is not enough. The challenge is not to help the laity to get tuned in on the church's monolog, but to prepare them for dialog and even confrontation with the powers at play in their secular callings. A report from an assembly of the World Council of Churches reads: "The real battles of the faith today are being fought in factories, shops, offices, and farms, in political parties and government agencies, in countless homes, in the press, radio, and television, in the relationship of nations. Very often it is said that the church should go into these spheres; but the fact is that the church is already in these spheres in the persons of its laity."

Pastors must be careful that they do not pull the laity off their secular base of operation, or make them feel guilty for not spending more time in church. Pastors are servants of the servants of God in the world. Often, however, the laity get the impression from their pastoral leaders that the big battle is for bigger budgets, higher attendance, increased membership, efficient kitchens, and other status symbols. The modern tragedy of the church has been the fallacy of a misplaced emphasis on itself, inevitably downgrading the dignity of the secular ministries of laity in the world. Sociologists of religion have been telling us that the church is scarcely making a dent on the mammoth structures of modern society. Instead, the reverse is happening; the church is succumbing to the erosive acids of secularism in aping the spirit, methods, and goals of the world. In this situation of the church's captivity, there is no more hopeful sign than a reawakened interest in the secular ministries of the laity. The social irrelevance of the church cannot be overcome by a preachers' church. Only the laity, not their pastors, can bring the church into the world's arenas. However, pastors can pave the way through right preaching and teaching. Only the laity can proclaim the lordship of Christ on the other side of the wall of partition built up between the secular and religious spheres. The way to recover the lay apostolate is not by making laity more active in preaching and liturgy, but by liberating them to become the church at work in the world. The current movement of trying to bring more lay people into church headquarters and to apply quotas for the internal organization of the church is a mere sop to the laity. It does nothing to revitalize the ministries of the laity in the world. A good lay person is not a junior grade pastor.

The unresolved issue is how to renew the laity for their ministries in the world? How can they become the church in the world? It can happen at the local congregational level through effective pastoral leadership. More often, however, the task is too large for one congregation. Lay institutes and schools of theology operated by clusters of congregations, districts, or synods, could be a step in the right direction. The aim of these schools would be to prepare church members for extra-parochial activities in society. The institutional church must overcome its tendency to lavish all its education on itself.

What resources does the church have to offer for the modern challenge of urbanization? The urban impact on the psychological and social patterns of life invades the life of every individual and family: crowded conditions, intense loneliness, political corruption, vast slums, increasing delinquency, teenage gangs, the crime wave, mental breakdown, suicide, class conflicts, dereliction, drugs and alcohol addiction, the divorce rate, business competition, pace of life. What does it mean to be a Christian in the midst of these realities? How is the church's preaching and teaching relevant to the ways of life in the city, based as it is on impersonal and anonymous relations, the ticking of the clock, the hectic schedules of a mass transportation system, the galloping rate of automation, and the rising tide of unemployment? How are these ingredients of urban life shaping the way in which church leaders are equipping laity for their mission and ministry in the world?

The career of the church has always been bound up with the city. Even in biblical times paradise was symbolized by a city, the New Jerusalem and Zion. In the ancient church Christianity spread first in the great urban centers of population in the Roman Empire. The word *pagan* referred to those living in the country. Obviously, the converts came from the cities. The task of the church today is to interpret the meaning of the kingdom under the conditions of constructing human communities in modern cities. The task is to demonstrate how a *koinonia* of grace can be established at the heart of everyday life in the city, how the sacred can be embodied in a secularized society, how worship can be allied with work, how a neighborhood can become a community in which justice and reconciliation can be experienced, how the relations between consumers and producers, employers and employees, whites and blacks and browns and yellows and reds and all the colors of the rainbow can be gathered up into a truly human community in which persons are treated as ends in themselves.

The pattern has been for the institutional church to retreat from urban centers. When life in the city has gotten too hot, the good shepherd has led his flock into the green pastures of the suburbs. It is always a scandal when a shift in the human chemistry of a neighborhood is permitted to drive the gospel out.

The pastor will stay with the congregation, equipping it to serve the victims of urban life: the orphans, the destitute, sick, feebleminded, insane, poor, aging people. Together they must deal with the individual victims of urban life, but more is required. They must go deeper into the underlying causes, challenge the powers that be, and move on group centers of decision to change the prevailing conditions. This involves social analysis and action. The pastor can at best be a catalyst and a facilitator in a community, engage in prophetic instruction, and proclaim the judgment of God against evil trends and forces. The Reverend Jesse Jackson of Operation PUSH has provided one model for how this can be done. His preaching is secular and political, though richly colored by biblical images. He mobilizes his troops to deal with *housing*: discrimination, restrictive covenants, zoning patterns, etc. He deals with *education*: its quality, financial support, de facto segregation, etc. He deals with *employment*: discriminatory practices, unemployment, chiefly among the unskilled, especially teenage blacks. He deals with city, state, national, and even international *politics*: voter registration, issues of war and peace, nuclear armaments, Reaganomics, etc.

Jesse Jackson's political type of ministry might be difficult for the average residential parish to emulate. Perhaps more nonresidential congregations ought to be formed. Many people do not feel at home in a typical family-centered style of parish. They do not necessarily dream of owning a house in a suburb with a two-car garage, a spouse, and several children in a family nest. As issue-oriented people they focus more on what they are *doing* than on where they are *living*. If the church is to be serious about renewing the ministry of the laity, it will be open to new structures equal to the complexities and mobilities of urban life.

NOTES

Chapter 1

1. Quoted by Gerhard Ebeling, *Luther: An Introduction to His Thought,* trans. R. A. Wilson (Philadelphia: Fortress Press, 1970), p. 248.
2. Walther von Loewenich, *Luther's Theology of the Cross,* trans. Herbert J. A. Bouman (Minneapolis: Augsburg Publishing House, 1976).
3. Ibid., p. 18.
4. Ibid., p. 23.
5. Cited in the *Formula of Concord,* Solid Declaration, Article 8, "The Person of Christ," *The Book of Concord,* trans. and ed. Theodore G. Tappert (Philadelphia: Fortress Press, 1959), p. 599.
6. Eberhard Jüngel, *God as the Mystery of the World: On the Foundation of the Theology of the Crucified One in the Dispute between Theism and Atheism,* trans. Darrell L. Guder (Grand Rapids, Mich.: Wm. B. Eerdmans Publishing Co., 1983).
7. Ibid., p. 35.
8. Jürgen Moltmann, *The Crucified God: The Cross of Christ as the Foundation and Criticism of Christian Theology,* trans. R. A. Wilson and John Bowden (New York: Harper & Row, 1974).
9. Ibid., p. 4.
10. Ibid., p. 205.
11. Ibid., p. 241.
12. Dietrich Bonhoeffer, *Letters and Papers from Prison,* trans. Reginald H. Fuller (New York: The Macmillan Co., 1953), pp. 219-220.
13. Kazoh Kitamori, *Theology of the Pain of God* (Richmond, Va.: John Knox Press, 1965).
14. Elie Wiesel, *Night* (New York: Hill and Wang, 1969), p. 44.
15. Walter Kasper, *Jesus the Christ,* trans. V. Green (New York: Paulist Press, 1976), p. 180.
16. Jon Sobrino, *Christology at the Crossroads,* trans. John Drury (Maryknoll, N.Y.: Orbis Books, 1978), p. 224.
17. Ibid., p. 225.
18. Karl Rahner, *The Trinity,* trans. Joseph Donceel (New York: Herder and Herder, 1970), p. 22.
19. Walther von Loewenich, *Luther's Theology of the Cross,* pp. 52ff.
20. Martin Luther, *The Freedom of a Christian,* in *Luther's Works,* vol. 31 (Philadelphia: Fortress Press, 1957), pp. 327ff.

21. *Luther's Works,* vol. 48 (Philadelphia: Fortress Press, 1963), p. 120.
22. *Luther's Works,* 48:281-282.
23. Karl Rahner, *Foundations of Christian Faith,* trans. William V. Dych (New York: The Seabury Press, 1978), p. 365.
24. "Message of the Assembly," in *Messages of the Helsinki Assembly,* The Lutheran World Federation (Minneapolis: Augsburg Publishing House, 1963), p. 121.
25. Karl Barth, *Church Dogmatics,* IV/1: 530.
26. These *coram* relationships are discussed by Ebeling, *Luther,* pp. 199-202.
27. Jürgen Moltmann, *The Crucified God,* p. 317.
28. Ibid., p. 318.
29. Douglas John Hall, *Lighten Our Darkness: Toward an Indigenous Theology of the Cross* (Philadelphia: Westminster Press, 1975), p. 32.
30. Ibid., p. 33.
31. Ibid., p. 146.
32. Ibid., p. 152.
33. Ibid., p. 151.
34. Ibid.
35. See the volume of essays on the Melbourne Conference of the Commission on World Mission and Evangelism of the World Council of Churches, *Witnessing to the Kingdom,* ed. Gerald H. Anderson (Maryknoll, N.Y.: Orbis Books, 1982).
36. Juan Luis Segundo has an unpublished but widely circulated public lecture on "The Shift within Latin American Theology."

Chapter 2

1. Cf. Ernst Troeltsch, *Die Absolutheit des Christentums und die Religionsgeschichte,* 2nd ed. (Tübingen, 1912).
2. Schubert Ogden, "Introduction," *Existence and Faith: Shorter Writings of Rudolf Bultmann* (New York: Meridian Books, Inc., 1960), pp. 20-21.
3. Paul Tillich, *Systematic Theology,* vol. 1 (The University of Chicago Press, 1951), p. 50.
4. Karl Rahner, "Anonymous Christians," *Theological Investigations* (Baltimore: Helicon Press, 1966), 6:390-395.
5. Cf., Walter Kasper, *Jesus the Christ,* trans. V. Green (New York: Paulist Press, 1976); Hans Küng, *On Being a Christian,* trans. Edward Quinn (Garden City, N.Y.: Doubleday & Company, 1976); Edward Schillebeeckx, *Jesus: An Experiment in Christology,* trans. Hubert

Hoskins (New York: The Seabury Press, 1979), and *Christ: The Experience of Jesus as Lord,* trans. John Bowden (New York: The Crossroad Publishing Company, 1981).

6. Cf. Gustavo Gutierrez, *A Theology of Liberation,* trans. Sister Caridad Inda and John Eagleson (Maryknoll, N.Y.: Orbis Books, 1973); John Sobrino, *Christology at the Crossroads,* trans. John Drury (Maryknoll, N.Y.: Orbis Books, 1978); Leonardo Boff, *Jesus Christ Liberator,* trans. Patrick Hughes (Maryknoll, N.Y.: Orbis Books, 1978).

7. Cf. Paul Knitter's study of Paul Althaus' theology, *Towards a Protestant Theology of Religions: A Case Study of Paul Althaus and Contemporary Attitudes* (Marburg: N. G. Elwert Verlag, 1974).

8. Hendrik Kraemer, *The Christian Message in a Non-Christian World* (New York: Harper, 1938); J. C. Hoekendijk, *The Church Inside Out,* trans. Isaac C. Rottenberg (Philadelphia: Westminster Press, 1966).

9. Gene TeSelle, *Christ in Context* (Philadelphia: Fortress Press, 1975).

10. James M. Gustafson, *Ethics from a Theocentric Perspective* (Chicago: The University of Chicago Press, 1981).

11. Ibid., p. 108.

12. The Christological section in Gustafson's book amounts to about four pages. The scanty attention paid to Christology is not, however, the chief problem. It is rank Ebionitism the like of which theology has scarcely seen since the time of English deism and New England unitarianism. Consider this view of the incarnation: "Jesus incarnates theocentric piety and fidelity" (p. 276). "The only good reason for claiming to be Christian is that we continue to be empowered, sustained, renewed, informed, and judged by Jesus' incarnation of theocentric piety and fidelity" (p. 277). It is piety and fidelity that get "incarnated," but what is meant is "exemplified."

13. John Hick, ed., *The Myth of God Incarnate* (Philadelphia: Westminster Press, 1977).

14. Tom F. Driver, *Christ in a Changing World* (New York: The Crossroad Publishing Company, 1981).

15. Rosemary Radford Ruether, *Faith and Fratricide: The Theological Roots of Anti-Semitism* (New York: The Seabury Press, 1974).

16. Cf. Paul Knitter, "Towards a Theocentric/Nonnormative Christology: Growing Endorsement," a paper delivered at the American Academy of Religion.

17. Paul Tillich, "The Significance of the History of Religions for the Systematic Theologian," *The Future of Religions* (New York: Harper & Row, 1966).

18. Cf. Wolfhart Pannenberg, "Toward a Theology of the History of Re-
    ligions," *Basic Questions in Theology,* trans. George H. Kehm (Phil-
    adelphia: Fortress Press, 1971), vol. 2.
19. Schubert M. Ogden, *The Point of Christology* (New York: Harper &
    Row, 1981); David R. Griffin, *A Process Christology* (Philadelphia:
    Westminster Press, 1973). Griffin makes the point that the resurrection
    of Jesus should be considered optional for modern Christians because
    it is both irrelevant to the essence of the Christian message and un-
    believable in terms of modern ways of thinking.
20. Pinchas Lapide, *The Resurrection of Jesus,* trans. Wilhelm Linss, with
    an introduction by Carl E. Braaten (Minneapolis: Augsburg Publishing
    House, 1983).
21. Franz Rosenzweig, *The Star of Redemption,* trans. William W. Hallo
    (New York: Holt, Rinehart and Winston, 1970), p. 396.

Chapter 3

1. Ed. Paul D. Opsahl and Marc H. Tannenbaum (Philadelphia: Fortress
   Press, 1974).
2. See Paul van Buren, *Discerning the Way: A Theology of the Jewish
   Christian Reality* (New York: The Seabury Press, 1980); Rosemary
   Radford Ruether, *Faith and Fratricide: The Theological Roots of Anti-
   Semitism* (New York: The Seabury Press, 1979).
3. Friedrich Schleiermacher, *The Christian Faith,* trans. H. R. Mack-
   intosh and J. S. Stewart (Edinburgh: T. & T. Clark, 1928), p. 60.
4. These sentences were written by Harnack in 1921 in his famous book
   on Marcion, and are here quoted from Helmut Gollwitzer, *An Introduction to Protestant Theology,* trans. David Cairns (Philadelphia: The
   Westminster Press, 1982), p. 126).
5. See Eva Fleischner, *Judaism in German Christian Theology since
   1945: Christianity and Israel Considered in Terms of Mission* (Me-
   tuchen, N.J.: The Scarecrow Press, 1975), pp. 44-50.
6. See Eva Fleischner, ibid., pp. 53-68, a chapter on "Jewish Christians."
7. K. H. Rengstorf, "The Place of the Jew in the Theology of the Christian Mission," *Lutheran World* 11 (1964): 279-295.
8. Karl Barth, *Church Dogmatics* (Edinburgh: T. & T. Clark, 1957), II/
   2: 228.
9. *Lutheran World,* 13.1 (1966): 66.
10. See the two volumes, *Der Ungekündigte Bund: Neue Begegnung von
    Juden und christlicher Gemeinde,* ed. Dietreich Goldschmidt and

Hans-Joachim Kraus (Stuttgart: Kreuz Verlag, 1962), and *Das Gespaltene Gottesvolk,* ed. Helmut Gollwitzer and Eleonore Sterling (Stuttgart: Kreuz Verlag, 1968).

11. Wolfhart Pannenberg, *Jesus—God and Man,* trans. Lewis L. Wilkins and Duane A. Priebe (Philadelphia: Westminster Press, 1968), pp. 254-255.

12. See *Judentum und Christentum—Einheit und Unterschied,* a dialog between Pinchas Lapide and Wolfhart Pannenberg (Munich: Chr. Kaiser Verlag, 1982).

13. Krister Stendahl, ''Judaism and Christianity II—After a Colloquium and a War,'' *Harvard Divinity Bulletin,* New Series 1 (Autumn, 1967): 5.

14. Franz Rosenzweig, *The Star of Redemption,* trans. William W. Hallo (New York: Holt, Rinehart and Winston, 1970), pp. 396, 397.

15. Pinchas Lapide, *Israelis, Jews, and Jesus,* trans. Peter Heinegg (Garden City, N.Y.: Doubleday & Co., 1979), pp. 31-32.

16. Quoted by Eva Fleischner, *Judaism in German Christian Theology since 1945,* p. 128.

17. *Jewish Monotheism and Christian Trinitarian Doctrine: A Dialogue by Pinchas Lapide and Jürgen Moltmann* (Philadelphia: Fortress Press, 1981), pp. 72-73.

18. Ibid., p. 81.

19. Ibid., p. 85.

20. Alfred Loisy, *The Gospel and the Church,* trans. Christopher Home (Philadelphia: Fortress Press, 1976), p. xxxvii.

21. Franz Rosenzweig, *The Star of Redemption,* p. 341.

22. Proclamation, ethical instruction, worship, tradition, and works of service.

Chapter 4

1. Arthur F. Glasser and Donald McGavran, *Contemporary Theologies of Mission* (Grand Rapids, Mich.: Baker Book House, 1983), p. 26.

2. Ibid., p. 27.

3. Ibid., pp. 101-107.

4. Ibid., pp. 65-77.

5. Ibid., pp. 69-70.

6. Ibid., p. 180.

7. Ibid., p. 182.

8. Simon E. Smith, ''Toward a New Missiology for the Church,'' *International Bulletin of Missionary Research* 6 (1982): 72.

9. Ibid.

10. Cf. *The New Face of Evangelicalism: An International Symposium on the Lausanne Covenant,* ed. C. Rene Padilla (Downers Grove, Ill.: InterVarsity Press, 1976). See also Orlando E. Costas, *Christ Outside the Gate: Mission Beyond Christendom* (Maryknoll, N.Y.: Orbis Books, 1982) and *The Integrity of Mission* (New York: Harper & Row, 1979).

11. See my book on Lutheran confessional principles, *Principles of Lutheran Theology* (Philadelphia: Fortress Press, 1983).

12. Quoted by Werner Elert, *The Structure of Lutheranism,* trans. Walter A. Hansen (St. Louis: Concordia Publishing House, 1962), p. 389.

13. Large Catechism, in *The Book of Concord,* ed. Theodore G. Tappert (Philadelphia: Fortress Press, 1959), pp. 426-427.

14. Ibid.

15. For an illuminating discussion of the history of Lutheranism's approach to mission and evangelism, see James Scherer's book, *"That the Gospel May Be Sincerely Preached throughout the World," A Lutheran Perspective on Mission and Evangelism in the 20th Century,* LWF Report 11/12, November, 1982 (published on behalf of the Lutheran World Federation, Geneva, Switzerland; Stuttgart: Kreuz Verlag Erich Breitsohl).

Chapter 5

1. Orlando E. Costas, *Christ Outside the Gate, Mission Beyond Christendom* (Maryknoll, N.Y.: Orbis Books, 1982).

2. W. A. Visser't Hooft, "Evangelism in the Neo-pagan Situation," *International Review of Mission* 65 (1976): 83.

3. Ibid., p. 83.

4. What I have to say about Christianity as an eschatological faith in these paragraphs and its meaning for the critique and construction of world history has been developed at length in a number of monographs, most notably, *The Future of God: The Revolutionary Dynamics of Hope* (New York: Harper & Row, 1969); *Christ and Counter-Christ: Apocalyptic Themes in Theology and Culture* (Philadelphia: Fortress Press, 1972); *Eschatology and Ethics* (Minneapolis: Augsburg Publishing House, 1974); *The Flaming Center* (Philadelphia: Fortress Press, 1977).

5. Fred L. Polak, *The Image of the Future* (New York: Oceana Publications, 1961), 2:44.

6. Karl Jaspers and Rudolf Bultmann, *Myth and Christianity* (New York: The Noonday Press, 1958).

7. Karl Barth, *The Epistle to the Romans,* trans. Edwyn C. Hoskyns (Oxford University Press, 1933), p. 314.

8. The current fashion in some circles is called "deconstruction." It is an intellectual movement that began in the field of literary criticism (Jacques Derrida) and has made its way via philosophy into theology. It is now the home base of the "God-is-dead" theology that is rooted in Nietzsche and reaches a form of eschatological nihilism in the thought of Thomas J. J. Altizer. Deconstruction in theology writes a good obituary for the amalgamated Christianity whose demise we have traced, but it offers no hope, no way forward, no signals of good news. Cf. Thomas J. J. Altizer, Max A. Myers, Carl A. Raschke, Robert P. Scharlemann, Mark C. Taylor, and Charles E. Winquist, *Deconstruction and Theology* (New York: Crossroad, 1982).

9. Karl Heim, *Jesus der Weltvollender* (Berlin: 1939), p. 172.

10. From Wolfhart Pannenberg, "Churchless Christians," *The Church,* trans. Keith Crim (Philadelphia: The Westminster Press, 1983), p. 9.

Chapter 6

1. Gustavo Gutierrez, *A Theology of Liberation* (Maryknoll, N.Y.: Orbis Books, 1973).

2. David Tracy, *Blessed Rage for Order: The New Pluralism in Theology* (New York: The Seabury Press, 1975).

3. Ibid., p. 245.

4. Ibid., p. 246.

5. Matthew L. Lamb, *Solidarity with Victims: Toward a Theology of Social Transformation* (New York: Crossroad, 1982).

6. Quoted in Richard Rubenstein, *Praxis and Action* (University of Pennsylvania Press, 1971), p. xi.

7. Karl Marx, *Contribution to the Critique of Hegel's Philosophy of Right,* ed. and trans. T. B. Bottomore (McGraw Hill, 1964), p. 52.

8. Ibid., p. 50.

9. Gutierrez, *A Theology of Liberation,* pp. 6-15.

10. Jürgen Moltmann, *Religion, Revolution and the Future* (New York: Charles Scribner's Sons, 1969), p. 138.

11. Johannes B. Metz, *Theology of the World* (New York: Herder & Herder, 1969), p. 112.

12. Carl E. Braaten, "Theory and Praxis: Reflections on an Old Theme," *Eschatology and Ethics* (Minneapolis: Augsburg Publishing House, 1974), p. 141.
13. 1 John 1:6, in the Greek.
14. See Jürgen Habermas, *Theory and Practice,* trans. John Viertel (Boston: Beacon Press, 1968) and also *Knowledge and Human Interests* (Boston: Beacon Press, 1971).
15. Hiram Caton, "Marx's Sublation of Philosophy into Praxis," *Review of Metaphysics* 26 (December, 1972): 233ff.
16. Kostas Axelos, *Alienation, Praxis, and Techne in the Thought of Karl Marx* (University of Texas Press, 1976), p. 285.
17. Gutierrez, *A Theology of Liberation,* p. 18.
18. Ibid., p. 46.
19. Marx wrote his response to Stirner in *The German Ideology,* attempting to show how he could escape the charge of being an idealist. If you have a reason to change the world before the fact, it would seem you are moving from an ideal plane beyond the concreteness of history itself, in the mode of an anticipating imagination or meaningful vision.
20. Wolfhart Pannenberg, *Theology and the Philosophy of Science,* trans. Francis McDonagh (Philadelphia: The Westminster Press, 1976), p. 96.
21. Jürgen Habermas, *Zur Logik der Sozialwissenschaften* (Frankfurt: 1971).
22. Pannenberg, *Theology and the Philosophy of Science,* p. 202.
23. Ibid., p. 196.
24. Ibid., p. 203.
25. *Witnessing to the Kingdom: Melbourne and Beyond,* ed. Gerald H. Anderson (Maryknoll, N.Y.: Orbis Books, 1982).
26. See Wolfhart Pannenberg's essay, "Der Sozialismus—das Wahre Gottesreich?" in *Müssen Christen Sozialisten sein?* ed. Wolfgang Teichert (Hamburg: Lutherisches Verlagshaus, 1976).
27. Wolfhart Pannenberg, "Faith and Disorder in Bangalore," *Worldview* 22 (March, 1979): 38.
28. Ibid.
29. Ibid.

Chapter 7

1. Cf. *The Identity of the Priest,* ed. Karl Rahner (*Concilium,* vol. 43; New York: Paulist Press, 1969).
2. *The Christian Century* 76.23 (June 10, 1959): 698-701.

3. Ibid., 700.
4. David S. Schuller, Merton P. Strommen, and Milo L. Brekke, *Ministry in America* (San Francisco: Harper & Row, 1980), p. 4.
5. Raymond E. Brown, *Priest and Bishop: Biblical Reflections* (New York: Paulist Press, 1970), p. 13.
6. John McKenzie, "Ministerial Structures in the New Testament," in *The Plurality of Ministries,* ed. Hans Küng and Walter Kasper (*Concilium,* vol. 74; New York: Herder & Herder, 1972), pp. 13-22.
7. Robert Clyde Johnson, "The Doctrine of the Ministry," *The Church and Its Changing Ministry,* ed. Robert Clyde Johnson (Philadelphia: The United Presbyterian Church USA, 1961), p. 100.
8. Edward Schillebeeckx, *Ministry, Leadership in the Community of Jesus Christ,* trans. John Bowden (New York: Crossroad, 1981).
9. Hans von Campenhausen, *Ecclesiastical Authority and Spiritual Power in the Church of the First Three Centuries,* trans. J. A. Baker (London: Adam & Charles Black, 1969), p. 27.
10. Ibid., p. 24.
11. John Naisbitt, *Megatrends: Ten New Directions Transforming Our Lives* (New York: Warner Books, 1982), p. 97.
12. Ibid., p. 189.

Chapter 8

1. For responsible scholarly treatments of Luther's views on the church, ministry, ordination, and succession, see the following works: J. Heubach, *Die Ordination zum Amt der Kirche* (Berlin, 1956); W. Brunotte, *Das geistliche Amt bei Luther* (Berlin, 1959); H. Lieberg, *Amt und Ordination bei Luther und Melanchthon* (Göttingen, 1962); Brian Gerrish, "Priesthood and Ministry in the Theology of Luther," *Church History* 34.4 (December 1965).
2. In his classic work, *The Lutheran Pastor,* G. H. Gerberding writes about the shaky foundations the Lutheran church has found in Luther's theology, and appeals instead to the much firmer foundations in the later theologians of Lutheran orthodoxy, particularly Chemnitz, Baier, Hollaz, and Gerhard.
3. For an account of these disputes, see James Lewis Schaaf, *Wilhelm Löhe's Relation to the American Church* (Inaugural Dissertation, Heidelberg University, 1961).
4. Hans Küng, *Structures of the Church* (New York: Thomas Nelson & Sons, 1964), p. 143.

5. Philip Melanchthon, Apology of the Augsburg Confession, *The Book of Concord*, ed. Theodore G. Tappert (Philadelphia: Fortress Press, 1959), p. 212.

6. Ibid.

7. *Eucharist and Ministry: Lutherans and Catholics in Dialogue*, vol. 4, published by U.S.A. National Committee of the Lutheran World Federation and the Bishops' Committee for Ecumenical and Interreligious Affairs (New York, 1960; reprinted by Augsburg Publishing House, 1979), p. 9.

8. Ibid., p. 27.

9. Ibid., p. 31.

10. *Unity in Faith and Life*, The Joint Theological Commission of the Church of South India and the Federation of Evangelical Lutheran Churches in India (Madras: The Christian Literature Society, 1955), p. 81.

11. Edmund Schlink, "Apostolic Succession," in *The Coming Christ and the Coming Church* (Philadelphia: Fortress Press, 1967), p. 232.

12. *The Historic Episcopacy*, ed. K. M. Carey (London: Dacre Press, 1954), pp. 21-22.

13. Karl Barth, *Church Dogmatics* IV. 2 (Edinburgh: T. & T. Clark, 1958), pp. 676f.

14. Robert C. Johnson, *The Church and Its Changing Ministry* (Philadelphia: The United Presbyterian Church in the U.S.A., 1961), p. 21.

15. Ibid., p. 22.

16. Ibid., p. 30.

17. Ibid., p. 40.

18. For a summary and evaluation of the Blake-Pike proposal, see *The Challenge to Reunion*, and particularly Robert M. Brown's essay, "Whence and Whither" (New York: McGraw-Hill Book Co., 1963).

19. An excellent survey of the COCU story is that of Gerald F. Moede, *Oneness in Christ: The Quest and the Questions* (Princeton, New Jersey: Minute Press, 1981).

20. P. C. Rodger and Lukas Vischer, eds. *The Fourth World Conference on Faith and Order* (New York: Association Press, 1964).

21. Ibid., p. 19.

22. *Baptism, Eucharist and Ministry*, Faith and Order Paper No. 111 (Geneva: World Council of Churches, 1982), paragraph 40 of the Ministry section.

23. Ibid., paragraph 41.

24. Ibid., paragraph 43.

Chapter 9

1. Luther's explanation of the Third Article of the Apostles' Creed, Small Catechism.
2. William Stringfellow, *A Private and Public Faith* (Grand Rapids, Mich.: William B. Eerdmans Publishing Company), p. 16.
3. Quoted by Gustaf Wingren, *The Living Word,* trans. Victor C. Pogue (Philadelphia: Muhlenberg Press, 1960), p. 64.
4. *Baptism, Eucharist and Ministry,* Faith and Order Paper No. 111 (Geneva: World Council of Churches, 1982), p. 10, paragraph 1.
5. Luther's explanation of the sacrament of Baptism, Small Catechism.
6. Paul Tillich, *Systematic Theology,* vol. 1 (Chicago: The University of Chicago Press, 1951), p. 3.
7. Gustaf Aulén, *The Faith of the Christian Church,* trans. Eric H. Wahlstrom (Philadelphia: Fortress Press, 1960), p. 318.
8. Paul Tournier, *The Whole Person in a Broken World* (New York: Harper & Row, 1964), p. 38.
9. Ivan Illich, *Medical Nemesis* (New York: Random House, 1976).
10. Hendrik Kraemer, *A Theology of the Laity* (Philadelphia: Westminster Press, 1958).